Presented to:

_____

By:

_____

On the Occasion of:

_____

Date:

_____

Truth.
Seeing Black and White in a Gray World

BARBOUR
PUBLISHING

For each truth revealed by grace, and received with inward delight and joy, is a secret murmur of God in the ear of a pure soul.

WALTER HILTON

INTRODUCTION

You face the questions every time someone sees you doing what is right. "Why would God want your money?" "Are you sure you should forgive someone who did *that?*" Each time someone questions your actions or decisions, you realize God's truth is often diametrically opposed to what the world believes to be true or wise.

Truth. will help you better understand the difference between God's way and the world's way. It's important to be able to answer questions for others, but it is even more important to be able to answer questions in your own heart.

God bless you in your search for the pure and simple truth, pulling away the gray veil of uncertainty and focusing on the *Truth.* It has always been there, and now you will see it as God sees it—defined by the light.

> *Truth is true—even if no one knows it.*
> *Truth is true—even if no one admits it.*
> *Truth is true—even if no one agrees with it.*
> *Truth is true—even if no one follows it.*
> *Truth is true—even if no one but God grasps it fully.*

PAUL COPAN

THE WORLD SAYS:
"If it feels good, do it."

GOD SAYS:
*"Do good,
even when it feels bad."*

Turn from evil and do good; then you will dwell in the land forever.
Psalm 37:27

Your five senses can give you fairly accurate messages most of the time. You can enjoy the coolness of a drink on a hot day, and it is good. You can enjoy the taste of ice cream and the wonderful scent of a flower. But your five senses are only a part of the information you need to be safe. Ask the diabetic about ice cream or one who is allergic about perfume. Or go deeper and ask the recovering drug addict or alcoholic about whether feelings are reliable guides.

Often this line, "If it feels good, do it," refers less to the abundant blessings life offers and more to using pleasure as a way to decide whether something should be done. If sex feels good, it follows by this reasoning that it should be done whenever possible and that the criteria of pleasure should guide your decisions. Not married? This reasoning says, "Go ahead if it feels good." Married, but not to the person you wish to have sex with? Go ahead if it feels good. When you follow pleasure as your main guide in such situations, the results are destroyed lives and relationships.

Doing what is right often moves against the grain of the world by requiring something that is inconvenient, costly, and sometimes life threatening. But that doesn't mean the Christian is against pleasure or that doing what is right is against pleasure.

C. S. Lewis once commented that humans are not guilty of seeking pleasure so much as they are guilty of settling too soon. We settle for earthly pleasures when we could hold out for the pleasures God promises us in His presence and in the provision He has made for our eternal life in heaven.

When the world encourages you to use pleasure as your guiding light, don't—look to God instead.

God made great and marvelous promises, so that his nature would become part of us. Then we could escape our evil desires and the corrupt influences of this world.

2 PETER 1:4 CEV

THE WORLD SAYS:
"Turn your back on those who wrong you."

GOD SAYS:
"Turn your back on the wrong and forgive those who wrong you."

"If you forgive those who sin against you, your heavenly Father will forgive you."
MATTHEW 6:14 NLT

How do you forgive someone who has murdered your child? How do you forgive someone who has shamed you in front of coworkers? How do you forgive someone who has stolen your purity or your dreams? The world says, "You can't and you shouldn't." Or they say, "It would be nice if you could, but I couldn't." And in some ways they are telling you the truth. They can't. It is impossible to overcome hatred, hurt, anger, and disappointment if you are trying to do it solely by human power.

One of the most perplexing things about the Christian life is that God expects the impossible and then asks for it! In teaching the disciples how to pray, Jesus said, "If you forgive others for their transgressions, your heavenly Father will also forgive you. But if you do not forgive others, then your Father will not forgive your transgressions" (Matthew 6:14–15 NASB). God forgives us freely, but He asks that we be a spendthrift with forgiveness in the same way.

The world is right when it says, "I can't forgive." But that's hardly the end of the matter. Everything changes when God comes into your life—you are changed and everything in your life shifts and moves to accommodate the new you. Forgiving those you could not forgive before is one of the supernatural signs that you are now a new person, cleansed by God and living by the power of the Holy Spirit.

If you have been crippled by unresolved anger and hurt, bound by unforgiveness toward someone in your life, go to God. Ask Him to touch your heart and change it. It's a prayer He has promised to answer, a miracle He is obliged to perform. Soon you will find yourself praying for that person and breathing in the pure air of freedom.

Jesus said, "Love your enemies and pray for those who persecute you, so that you may be children of your Father in heaven."

MATTHEW 5:44–45 NRSV

THE WORLD SAYS:
"If you are truly successful, others will serve you."

GOD SAYS:
"If you are truly successful, you will serve others."

Jesus said, "The greatest among you should be like the youngest, and the one who rules like the one who serves."

LUKE 22:26

There is something about being on top in the leadership position that attracts the world. Success is measured in terms of how many people you order around or how many thankless tasks you avoid. It is also measured in how much spotlight you garner in the public eye. All these things are worth something to the world, and if a person chooses a profession of service, their friends become concerned. "A schoolteacher? Well, later on you might want to become a principal. A nurse? Why not go ahead and become a doctor? A missionary? But you are so gifted! You could be so much more."

When God came among us as a human, one of the things He showed us was a servant's heart. And He showed us something else: It takes more strength, more self-esteem, and more faith to serve others than all that is required to lead. A minister once said that the way to tell if you have a servant's heart is if you aren't offended when people treat you like a servant.

Here is another place where God calls us to walk in ways that are humanly impossible without Him. Something happens to the Christian who spends time in God's presence every day—something miraculous. Faith increases, the heart grows more loving, and suddenly a new person begins to emerge who doesn't care who gets credit for things on earth because they know that God will notice everything at a time when it really counts.

How about you? Would you like to become a miracle in motion on the stage of life? Spend time with God and learn His heart by reading His Word. If you are patient, something wonderful will begin from the inside out—and it will feel a whole lot like success.

Serve wholeheartedly, as if you were serving the Lord, not men.
Ephesians 6:7

THE WORLD SAYS:
"Live for today."

GOD SAYS:
"Live for eternity."

A man came up to Jesus and asked, "Teacher, what good thing must I do to get eternal life?"

MATTHEW 19:16

The simple cross-stitch banner hung on the bathroom wall for years. It read, "One hundred years from now, it will not matter what kind of house I lived in, how much money I had, nor what my clothes were like. But the world will be a better place, because I was important in the life of a child." This statement really asks, "Are you living for today or are you investing in tomorrow?" Better put, it suggests, "Are you living for eternity?"

The Bible says all of us will live on after we die a physical death. Life on this earth is only the beginning of our existence. We will have an existence after we die with or without God. Yet, our eternal destination rests on some decisions we make here on Earth in this lifetime. Those who place their trust in Jesus as Lord will be raised to new life to live with Him forever. Those who reject the grace that could be theirs face eternal separation from God. In light of these realities, shouldn't we examine our priorities in the here and now?

Should our lives be about collecting possessions and riches, or trying to win others in love to an eternal life with God? Can we ignore God and His commands? Can we ignore the needs of other people? In reality, God placed you on this earth for a purpose. Through accepting Christ as your Lord and Savior, letting Him forgive you and live His life through you, and letting Him renew your mind to conform to His, you begin to live the life of an eternal being.

All we can take with us to heaven is our own soul and each other. Find out what pleases God. Find out what will matter one hundred, one thousand, or one million years from now and go do it!

This world is fading away, along with everything it craves.
But if you do the will of God, you will live forever.

1 John 2:17 nlt

TRUTH.

THE WORLD SAYS:
"I love you because..."

GOD SAYS:
"I love you in spite of..."

This is how God showed his love among us: He sent his one and only Son into the world that we might live through him. This is love: not that we loved God, but that he loved us and sent his Son as an atoning sacrifice for our sins.

1 JOHN 4:9–10

Unfailing love. Unconditional love. What a short supply we have today! Everybody wants it but few find it. A pat on the head goes to the good girl. A hug goes out to the obedient boy. But, what about the naughty boy or girl? Where is the love for them? And what about the drunkard or the criminal? Will they ever feel loved? Or, are they forever labeled: unworthy?

It doesn't matter how good or bad you are. God says He loves you no matter what you do. He says that His love for you isn't based on what you do, say, or believe. He doesn't love you because you made the grade or even because of your good deeds. He loves preachers, teachers, missionaries, prostitutes, drug dealers, sex offenders, liars, and cheaters—just the same. He loves you because He made you. He loves you because you are His.

What a profound and freeing thing this is. Let it sink down deep into the inner core of your being. God loves you in spite of your errors, sin, foibles, and character defects. This is a big reason why His grace is so amazing. Your boss, your spouse, and even your parents may turn their backs on you, withhold love from you, or even be rude and unkind to you. But God will never do that. God's love is perfect, constant, and unconditional.

The interesting thing is that because God loves you so profoundly, He has given you a free will—a will to choose if and when you will love Him in return. If you go to Him, He will receive you. If you reach out to Him, He will take your hand and never let you go. God's love is not based on your worthiness, but on your willingness. God loves you just the way you are. What will you do with His love?

How precious is your unfailing love, O God! All humanity finds shelter in the shadow of your wings.

PSALM 36:7 NLT

THE WORLD SAYS:
"It's impossible."

GOD SAYS:
"Nothing is impossible for Me."

Jesus looked at them and said, "With man this is impossible, but with God all things are possible."

MATTHEW 19:26

The wind raged. Large waves buffeted the tiny boat. Darkness covered the sea.

Far away in the distance, a tiny figure approached, walking on top of the water. The crew couldn't believe their eyes. They cried out in fear, thinking they were seeing a ghost. But, as the figure approached, He comforted the crew. Immediately, the disciples recognized this miracle worker. It was Jesus. One disciple asked, "Lord, if it's You, tell me to come to You on the water." Jesus said, "Come." In faith, Peter got out of the boat, put both feet down, and walked on water.

Powerless in his own strength, Peter's faith allowed him to do the miraculous. Moments later—defeated by doubt—Peter began to sink. Jesus rebuked Peter for his lack of faith and then took him by the hand and led him back to the boat. Prayer and faith are keys that unlock God's miraculous power to make possible what we perceive to be impossible.

After faith and prayer, God made the lame walk. He made the blind see. He raised a little girl and his friend Lazarus from the dead. Before any of us existed, He created the heavens, earth, and all life out of nothing. He died and rose again.

If God is all-powerful, and if He created all things, wouldn't He also have the power to change all things? Is it too difficult for Him to override expected operations of physical systems? All creation bows before His authority. He can reorder or reorganize creation anytime He chooses.

Therefore, the impossible is still possible today. Prayers are offered and cancers subside, financial needs are met, hard hearts soften and turn to Christ for salvation. Take a step of faith and walk out into the unknown. Believe God for the impossible.

I will show wonders in the heaven above and
signs on the earth below.

ACTS 2:19

THE WORLD SAYS:
"I'll believe it when I see it."

GOD SAYS:
"Blessed are those who believe without seeing."

Jesus told him, "You believe because you have seen me. Blessed are those who haven't seen me and believe anyway."

JOHN 20:29 NLT

Leaning back from his test tubes, hoses, and butane flames, the scientist shouted "Eureka. It's true!" After months of toil, the man in the white coat now knew that his theorem actually worked. The biochemical engineer observed precise quantifiable measurements. He saw a satisfactory outcome. The scientist needed to see to believe.

Are you like the man in the white coat? Do you need specific measurable evidence in order to believe God? Sometimes it's hard to see God at work, but He has already given us evidence of His presence and His goodness. History witnesses and records His involvement in human lives.

We read stories and hear testimonies of God continually reaching out with His love and goodness. He shows up in the middle of trouble. He sees injustice and provides relief. He orchestrates minor miracles (and sometimes large ones, too). The scientist might call it natural phenomenon.

What happened to Shadrach, Meshach, and Abednego was a phenomenon of a supernatural kind. These three Hebrew children refused to bow down to the golden god that King Nebuchadnezzar set up, and as a result, they were thrown into the fiery furnace. Evidence suggested they would die. Evidence suggested God wasn't good. Yet, these three men believed God to be their Helper, their Savior. On this principle they stood their ground. They believed God without knowing the outcome.

For their faith, they not only lived but walked out of the furnace unsinged! And the king praised God and gave them a promotion in his kingdom. Isn't it amazing what a little faith can do? Our faith isn't blind but is based on thousands of years of a just, faithful, and good God acting in human history. With so much evidence available to us, why not believe and trust in His name?

Jesus said: "Stop doubting and believe."
John 20:27

THE WORLD SAYS:
"The universe is the result of a cosmic accident."

GOD SAYS:
"I created the heavens and the earth."

The basic reality of God is plain enough. Open your eyes and there it is! By taking a long and thoughtful look at what God has created, people have always been able to see what their eyes as such can't see: eternal power, for instance, and the mystery of his divine being. So nobody has a good excuse.

ROMANS 1:19–20 MSG

Now more than ever, renowned scientists and scholars from major universities subscribe to the possibility of intelligent design as an explanation for the origin of the universe. Evolutionary theorists face a challenge from top minds on the idea of how the universe was created. Could there be a cause behind it all?

Who really knows what or who caused the big bang? Why is there any matter at all? How did it get here and why is it seemingly organized? Why are there solar systems? Why earth? Furthermore, why are there humans? Could it all have been created by chance? Since there were no witnesses to the origin of the universe, the best we can do is look at the evidence and draw our own conclusions.

Darwin's findings never really explored metaphysics and the question of human origins, but other scientists have taken his studies and created a whole godless paradigm for interpreting the meaning of all physical matter.

God, however, says you can see evidence of His handiwork in His creation. God says this evidence demands a response.

The implications of godless origins are enormous. If God didn't create the earth, or us, we have no responsibility to Him. If God didn't create Adam, then the concept of original sin is also erroneous. Jesus wouldn't have had to come and die for our sins. The whole premise of Christianity wouldn't hold up in a world created by chance.

When we look at the details of intelligent design and believe that God made us and the world, our response should be adoration, praise, and submission. The grandeur and vastness of the solar system and the complexities of microbial worlds all declare the glory of God. His power and might are on display everywhere. Can you see His intelligent design?

Everything comes from [God]; everything happens through him; everything ends up in him. Always glory! Always praise! Yes. Yes. Yes.

ROMANS 11:36 MSG

THE WORLD SAYS:
"Listen to your gut instincts."

GOD SAYS:
"Listen to the still, small voice of My Spirit within you."

Jesus said, "My sheep listen to my voice; I know them, and they follow me."
JOHN 10:27

Anyone who has been around sheep knows they aren't too bright. They eat grass and grain, bleat, and follow other sheep. Being called a sheep isn't a good thing. But right there in the middle of the Gospels, Christ calls His followers sheep. Some Christians might cringe and want to ignore that part of scripture. But, sheep have one very honorable quality: They are good listeners. They follow the voice and lead of their shepherd.

Imagine if one sheep said to another, "Our shepherd doesn't know what he's talking about. There is a better way to get to the good water and grass." The sheep's buddy might say, "You know, you might be right. Our shepherd is taking his time in getting us to the good stuff, and I'm hungry. Let's go your way." Such a position would ultimately lead to disaster. Sheep just don't know the way.

Christ is constantly looking out for you. He speaks to His people—His sheep—every day. He knows the way, and He knows what paths to avoid. He has the perspective of being God. He knows all history. He understands your entire DNA and personality completely. He is entirely trustworthy. That's why it's important to hear His voice. Other people might have a little bit of wisdom and experience, but God knows all. Your gut instinct might be only the pizza that you ate last night rumbling in you, but God has eternal perspective.

A good shepherd talks to his sheep. He walks ahead of them to help them find the safest path. Despite treacherous terrain, a shepherd takes his sheep to refreshing waters and open pastures for grazing. Are you listening to the Good Shepherd?

Christ often retreated into the hills to listen to His heavenly Father. It was crucial for His ministry and life. So follow His lead by stopping to listen.

Jesus said, "Blessed are they that hear the word of God, and keep it."
LUKE 11:28 KJV

THE WORLD SAYS:
"People are innately good."

GOD SAYS:
"All people are born with a rebellious heart."

The Lord saw how great man's wickedness on the earth had become, and that every inclination of the thoughts of his heart was only evil all the time.

Genesis 6:5

In ancient days, two brothers offered sacrifices to God. The Lord looked with favor on one offering but not on the other. This angered the brother with the unacceptable offering, and he followed his more acceptable brother to a remote spot and killed him. You've probably heard the story—Cain, Adam and Eve's son, attacked and murdered his brother Abel. This rebellious act was not the reflection of a violent society. Cain was born just one generation apart from parents who were created in divine perfection. But sin had obtained a foothold in the human race, and it was already rearing its ugly head.

Thousands of years later, mankind is no better off. We're stuck with the curse of sin. It's embedded in our very nature. It's a stain that won't rub off.

One might say, "I'm not a murderer. I'm basically a good person." But take a really hard, serious look at your heart. If you ever told one lie, you are a liar. If you ever said, "I don't need God. I have my own things," then you have practiced idolatry. God's Word says, "All have sinned and fall short of the glory of God" (Romans 3:23). This means Billy Graham, the Dali Lama, Bono, Mother Teresa, and you—this means everybody.

It's true. Humans are made in the image of God, male and female. There is a stamp of God's goodness and character indelibly imprinted in our bodies and spirits. When people act in line with God's character, they are responding to a love He first lavished on us, but that doesn't erase our sin natures. The only way to be truly clean is to accept the grace that comes by Christ Jesus. He paid a debt we couldn't pay to live a life we never had. Christ alone erases the old sinful man and gives us a new, holy life.

Just as by the one man's disobedience the many were made sinners, so by the one man's obedience the many will be made righteous.

ROMANS 5:19 NRSV

THE WORLD SAYS:
"The Bible is just a book."

GOD SAYS:
"The Bible is My inspired Word to you."

The word of God is living and active. Sharper than any double-edged sword, it penetrates even to dividing soul and spirit, joints and marrow; it judges the thoughts and attitudes of the heart.

HEBREWS 4:12

Read any good books lately? Pages turn fast in the latest best-sellers. Gripping novels keep readers wanting more. The best books inspire readers to change their lifestyles or beliefs. Few become legendary—classics for every generation. But only one book claims to be the inspired Word of God. That book is the best-selling book of all time: the Holy Bible.

A collection of historical tales, poems, songs, prophecy, genealogical records, parables and proverbs—sixty-six individual books in all make up its pages. Though many, many authors can lay claim to authorship, the Spirit of God inspired and spoke through these writers to create a document that lives and breathes. In a brilliant orchestration of thematic synergy, all books theologically agree as they paint an awesome portrait of a holy God revealing Himself through human history.

It's dangerous to seriously read the Bible. It challenges the reader to review his or her beliefs about everything. Evolutionists confront creationism. Haters find love. Anarchists find order. Liars find truth. And it tells people they must die and be born again. Every Bible reader must wrestle with the questions of Christ. Every Bible reader must decide whether Jesus really does take away the sin of the world—or not. This hot potato of a book makes incredible claims. Can these claims be true? The Bible will not let its readers be indifferent.

If the Bible is just a book, it can be forgotten. It can be disregarded, minimalized, and considered irrelevant. It becomes the flavor of the month—a fun summer read that loses influence or appeal with the passing of the seasons. If the Bible doesn't live up to its claims, it's really a bunch of lies or the collection of rants of some lunatics who didn't know what they were talking about. But if it's true…

Every part of Scripture is God-breathed and useful one way or another—showing us truth, exposing our rebellion, correcting our mistakes, training us to live God's way. Through the Word we are put together and shaped up for the tasks God has for us.

2 TIMOTHY 3:16–17 MSG

THE WORLD SAYS:
"Truth is relative."

GOD SAYS:
"I am Truth,
and I do not change."

Jesus answered, "I am the way and the truth and the life. No one comes to the Father except through me."

JOHN 14:6

The idea remains revolutionary. Truth is a Person.

It's easy to wrap your mind around Truth equaling plati-tudes or rules or statements, but a Person? How strange! If Truth equals these impersonal things, then they can be rein-terpreted over time. They can be applied differently under different circumstances. Or, they can be discarded altogether.

It's easy to ignore a piece of paper, a plaque on the wall, or even an engraving in stone with a neat saying. But it's hard to ignore a person—especially One with ultimate authority. After all, words cannot talk back or put up a fuss or imple-ment consequences. But a person? That's different. And, that Person is God.

Scripture gives indication of this phenomenon. It says, "God is not a man, that he should lie, nor a son of man, that he should change his mind" (Numbers 23:19). Hebrews 13:8 says, "Jesus Christ is the same yesterday and today and for-ever." This steady, unchanging nature of God has tremendous implications for us.

If God never changes, and if God equals truth, then truth never changes. This actually allows easy decision making. It's always wrong to lie because long ago, God said, "Do not lie" (see Exodus 20:16). It's always wrong to dishonor your par-ents because long ago, God said, "Honor your father and your mother" (Exodus 20:12).

When temptations come to violate these and other truths, you can always fall back on what you know to be true and holy. The more you know this God, the more you understand His standard of holiness. Furthermore, Christians have the personification of that standard giving them strength to resist temptation. God's your biggest cheerleader for daily living in holiness. God as truth—standard and cheerleader—stands on guard continually, empowering you with His Spirit, life, and friendship to live a life of truth.

Jesus said, "You will know the truth, and the truth will set you free."
JOHN 8:32

THE WORLD SAYS:
"Promises are made to be broken."

GOD SAYS:
"I will never break My promises to you."

God said, "I establish my covenant with you: Never again will all life be cut off by the waters of a flood; never again will there be a flood to destroy the earth."

GENESIS 9:11

"But, Dad, you promised." The dejected son looks mournfully to the ground. "You said you'd watch my game today." The father hems and haws and explains away why he cannot honor his word to his son. The father goes off to do his own thing, and the son grows up thinking that promises are meant to be broken.

Who hasn't been on the stinging end of a broken promise? It stinks! It hurts! And trust is compromised. Family members, coworkers, friends, and enemies all break promises. All relationships suffer when promises are broken.

Is there anybody who remains true to his or her word?

Consider God. Long ago He created a beautiful promise: the rainbow. This promise hasn't been broken for thousands of years. God established these great arches of red, orange, yellow, green, blue, indigo, and violet as a physical reminder of the strength of His Word. For thousands of years, God has never destroyed the earth with a flood again. This beautiful promise happens frequently and regularly all around the world. With the rainbow, God says, "I'm not only true, I'm trustworthy. I say what I mean, and I mean what I say."

In the Bible, God calls promises covenants—binding contracts between Him and His people. They are a record and a pronouncement of His faithfulness to humanity. God issued numerous covenants to humanity throughout Bible times, and His final covenant of forgiveness of sins through Christ remains in effect today.

Another time God says, "I will never break my covenant with you" (Judges 2:1). Psalm 105:8 says, "He remembers his covenant forever." If God fulfills a promise or covenant given thousands of years ago, will He not fulfill His promises today? Look closer. Can you see the signs of the promise of His love?

God is love. Whoever lives in love lives in God, and God in him. In this way, love is made complete among us so that we will have confidence on the day of judgment, because in this world we are like him.

1 John 4:16–17

THE WORLD SAYS:
"Miracles don't exist."

GOD SAYS:
"Lazarus, arise!"

Jesus said, "This sickness will not end in death. No, it is for God's glory so that God's Son may be glorified through it."

JOHN 11:4

Lazarus stunk—after all, he'd been dead and buried for four days when Jesus arrived. Lazarus's sisters Mary and Martha had summoned Jesus to come when Lazarus became ill, but He had been unwilling to leave the crowds of needy followers behind. Now the women greeted Jesus with sorrowful looks. They were sure it was too late. They were sure—but they were wrong. When He arrived, Jesus wept because He loved Lazarus very much. Then He asked for the stone to be removed from the tomb and called out in a loud voice, "Lazarus, come out!" The once-dead man, still wrapped in his grave clothes, came out before many witnesses.

God still performs miracles today—miracles that impact the physical, emotional, mental, and spiritual aspects of our lives. They run like threads through our daily existence: a wrong forgiven, a recovery from illness, unexpected income to meet a pressing financial need, a sinful heart restored to love and purity, a life estranged from God finding joy and peace in eternal relationship with Him. All these things are miracles. Look around and you'll see them, too. A truck-car collision where the passengers walk away without a scratch, the young soldier whose vehicle narrowly misses a roadside bomb, a good job turns up after months of unemployment.

Scoffers may tell you miracles don't happen. "Life stinks and then you die" seems to be the prevailing attitude of some. But ask God to open your eyes, and you'll never consider joining the ranks of the miracle debunkers.

When Jesus sent His disciples out into the world, He said, "Heal the sick, raise the dead, cleanse those who have leprosy, drive out demons" (Matthew 10:8). These commands have not been retracted. God has always—and still does—suspend the natural laws for our sake as He sees fit, whether we believe it—or not.

You are the God of miracles and wonders! You demonstrate your awesome power among the nations.

PSALM 77:14 NLT

THE WORLD SAYS:
"Love is a feeling."

GOD SAYS:
"Love is a decision."

Love is patient, love is kind. It does not envy, it does not boast,
it is not proud. It is not rude, it is not self-seeking,
it is not easily angered, it keeps no record of wrongs.

1 CORINTHIANS 13:4–5

The bride and groom vowed undying love. Each told the other that they would love each other "for richer or poorer, in sickness and in health, till death do us part." They knew that someday the babies would cry, the mortgage would be due, and the added pounds would come to their waistlines. But they decided that even in the most difficult moments, they would make a decision to love each other. It was the only way their love could last.

It is not necessary to feel love to act in love. How does the son love and honor the alcoholic father? How do you love the neighbor who plays loud music all night long or allows his dog to trample your flowerbed? What if your spouse commits adultery? Can you still love then? Feelings come and go, but a decision to love says, "In spite of how I'm feeling about you right now, I will act in love toward you."

Look again at the attributes of love from 1 Corinthians 13. Does it say "Love is giddy, love is warm. It's joyful all the time. It struts around like a peacock. It can be discarded when it's not fun anymore"? Of course not. Those things might be admiration, tenderness, or even strong feelings, but they aren't love.

Love has guts. It toughs things out. It recognizes moments of difficulty, when the warm fuzzies have turned to the cold pricklies. It forgives when one person in the relationship is being a bullheaded idiot. God offers real, nitty-gritty love to humanity. He has made a way for us to give it to others, too. That's the kind of love worth giving and receiving, because that's the love that will make it "for better or for worse."

Many waters cannot quench love; rivers cannot wash it away.
If one were to give all the wealth of his house for love,
it would be utterly scorned.

Song of Solomon 8:7

THE WORLD SAYS:
"Don't be 'holier than thou.'"

GOD SAYS:
"Be holy as I am holy."

Be imitators of God, therefore, as dearly loved children.
Ephesians 5:1

A 1980s pop-rock song has these lyrics: "Don't drink. Don't smoke. What do you do? Goody-two, Goody-two, goody-goody-two-shoes." The singer takes a mocking stance toward those who have set themselves apart from the rest of the crowd.

But, there is nothing wrong with being set apart from the crowd when it means you are set apart for God, and that's what holiness means. It's so much more than keeping your morals shined up. It's living a clean and free-enough life that the love and power of God can move in and through you.

Of course, it is possible to be "good for goodness' sake" alone. Such a strategy would even pay off in terms of keeping you out of trouble, avoiding guilt, and avoiding a bruised conscience and sleepless nights. But man-made holiness can never compare to the holiness that results from living for God.

Ultimately, God demands holiness for those who want to abide in His presence. He says in Hebrews 12:14, "Without holiness no one will see the Lord." He demands that because He knows it's the only way you can enter into His presence. He also knows that you could never clean yourself up well enough to approach Him on your own. That's why He asks that you cleanse yourself in the precious blood of His sinless Son, Jesus. In that way, you become holy by proxy and worthy to go before Him.

Once you have been cleansed and made holy, His Holy Spirit is present to help you stay that way. He will help you resist temptation, break old habits, find the grace to forgive others, and ask for forgiveness whenever the stain of sin has touched your life again. It's a good thing to be holy—no matter what anyone says. And God has made it possible for you to live in holiness before Him.

God did not call us to be impure, but to live a holy life.
1 THESSALONIANS 4:7

THE WORLD SAYS:
"Choose your own path."

GOD SAYS:
"Follow Me!"

Jesus said: "If anyone would come after me, he must deny himself and take up his cross daily and follow me."

LUKE 9:23

The Robert Frost poem says, "Two roads diverged in a yellow wood…and I took the one less traveled by, and that has made all the difference." Comparatively few travel the path of Christ. Choosing this path seems like foolishness to many. It stands diametrically opposed to conventional wisdom. The world says "Carve your own niche. Get ahead. Get rich." Others in the world say, "Easy does it. We're all brothers. I'm okay. You're okay." Materialism and open, extreme tolerance for sin and sinful lifestyles seem to be the leading competitors for the call of Christ.

The call of Christ is radical. It says, "Leave whatever you are doing and take a journey into unknown territory." It *doesn't* say, "Suppress yourself." It says, "Die to self."

The path of Christ says, "All that I am, do, and say is in God's service." It says, "My mandate is to love God and love my neighbor as myself." It says, "The material is temporary while the eternal is everlasting." It also says, "Be intolerant of sin and unrighteousness."

The call of Christ isn't some pious, boring life. It's a call to adventure, hope, and trust. It might lead you to foreign fields, or important halls of government, or media, or onto the poorest streets of America. God asks His travelers to have courage and strength, and then He offers to embolden and challenge His followers to love and be loved.

Unfortunately, all roads of our own choosing eventually lead to a dead end. But the road of Christ leads to life eternal. Will there be difficulties and struggles along the way? Undoubtedly. But Christ promises to always walk with us in the darkest valleys. He also offers joy, love, and peace. Can we find these commodities in communities where every man is out for himself? Come see the difference of the road less traveled.

It is the Lord your God you must follow, and him you must revere.
Deuteronomy 13:4

THE WORLD SAYS:
"There is nothing after this life."

GOD SAYS:
"In My kingdom, you will live forever."

To those who by persistence in doing good seek glory, honor and immortality, he will give eternal life.

ROMANS 2:7

In God's plan, mankind was meant to live forever. God made Adam and Eve and put them in a Garden to live in continual community with Him. If the two original humans had never sinned, we would still be enjoying their company today. Their sin, however, introduced death to the world. And now, all humankind suffers their same fate. Our human bodies are subject to the inevitability of death. But physical death is far from a final chapter. In fact, it is a new beginning.

Jesus Christ has upended the curse of sin and undone the damage resulting from Adam and Eve's poor choice. Through His death on the cross and His resurrection, He has made it possible for us to rejoin the kingdom of God. For those who choose to receive His sacrificial gift, death can conquer only the physical body. Their souls and spirits will live on eternally. And the loss of that old, flawed body is countered with the gift of a new, immortal body.

The details of our lives after death are known only in glimpses taken from scripture, but the surety of its superiority over life as we now know it is certain. We will be as we were intended—one with God, whole, and beyond the reach of this life's pain and tragedies. And we know that we will not be ghosts, trapped on the other side, longing to return to this world, and unable to let go of our lives here. We will be free! Our lives here on earth will finally be placed in perspective.

Death was never God's intention, and for those who come to understand that Jesus is the "way, the truth, and the life" (see John 14:6 NKJV), it is never the end. Rather, it is the point from which life flows out in every direction.

"Whoever believes in the Son has eternal life."
JOHN 3:36

THE WORLD SAYS:
"We have no power over death."

GOD SAYS:
"Death has no power over those who believe in Me."

Jesus said, "I tell you the truth, whoever hears my word and believes
him who sent me has eternal life and will not be condemned;
he has crossed over from death to life."

JOHN 5:24

The lady at the cosmetics counter said to her customer, "Try this vanishing cream. It'll make you look ten years younger." The customer liberally applied it, hoping the saleslady was right. She didn't want to look old. She didn't want to die. She wanted to remain forever young. Unfortunately, creams, tonics, vitamins, and exercise plans will not stave off death. Nothing on earth has the power to stop the inevitable.

The psalmist writes about the awful truth. "What man can live and not see death, or save himself from the power of the grave?" (Psalm 89:48).

What hope then is there for anyone? Can the power of death somehow be overthrown? Scripture tells us, "Yes!" Scripture says there is an answer! It says faith in Christ alone will destroy the power of death. Hosea 13:14 foretold of this power with these words: "I will ransom them from the power of the grave; I will redeem them from death." Christ clarifies this verse by saying, "I am the resurrection and the life. He who believes in me will live, even though he dies; and whoever lives and believes in me will never die" (John 11:25–26).

How then do we find power over death? How do we find eternal life? It's just plain, simple belief in Christ. Believe He is God. Believe you are a sinner. Believe He loves you. Believe He died for your sins. Believe He can offer you what no one else can—eternity in His presence.

Do you have doubts? Believe anyway. Faith says "I'll trust in You despite my doubts, regardless of my circumstances." Jesus waits—ready, willing, and able to eliminate the power of death in your life. Will your earthly body still age? Will it still wear out and be discarded. Of course! But a new body and a new life will be waiting for you in an instant.

Though outwardly we are wasting away, yet inwardly we are being renewed day by day. For our light and momentary troubles are achieving for us an eternal glory that far outweighs them all.

2 CORINTHIANS 4:16–17

THE WORLD SAYS:
"Put yourself first."

GOD SAYS:
"Put others first."

Do nothing out of selfish ambition or vain conceit,
but in humility consider others better than yourselves.

PHILIPPIANS 2:3

The Boy Scouts teach it. So do Sunday school teachers. So do many parents. It's "loving your neighbor"—and it seems to be in short supply these days. Help an old lady across the street. Open doors for others. Serve someone else the first slice of pie. More than just common courtesies, these acts represent tangible demonstrations of God's love. They give testimony to the reality of God's transforming power in our lives.

Jesus told the story of the Good Samaritan. A man was beaten up and left for dead on the side of the road. Important people, too busy to stop and help, walked on by. One man, however, a Samaritan, went the extra mile and bandaged the guy up, took him to a hotel, and paid for the room. Talk about going above and beyond the call of duty! This type of service should be normal operating behavior for the people of God.

Imagine a world where all people constantly serve each other and put each other first. Crime would dry up. No one would be in need. We would all be looking out for each other. That would be heaven, right? Why shouldn't we learn to walk in heaven's ways here on earth?

Leave plenty of space and time in your life to be of service to others. Stranded travelers and needy people need to see Jesus Christ with real flesh and bones. They need to see the love of Christ displayed in God's people who put others ahead of their own agendas. And, while you are taking care of others, God will take care of you—probably through the helping hands of other selfless servants. In the end, it's as simple as this: You can put others first because God put you first. He's the greatest servant of all, and He wants you to be just like Him.

This is how we know what love is: Jesus Christ laid down his life for us. And we ought to lay down our lives for our brothers.

1 JOHN 3:16

THE WORLD SAYS:
"There are many ways to heaven."

GOD SAYS:
"Only Jesus, My Son, made the sacrifice for your sins."

Jesus answered, "I am the way and the truth and the life. No one comes to the Father except through me."

JOHN 14:6

How good is good enough to get into heaven? If you work hard, raise a nice family, and give to charity, is that enough? Or do you have to become a missionary or give up the things you really want to please God enough to let you through the pearly gates? Or maybe you are going to have to live numerous lives in order to get "promoted" into heaven. And what about the Muslims, Hindus, and other religious practitioners? Don't all roads lead to God?

All religions are not the same. There are some profound, fundamental differences that cannot be ignored. Christianity is unique and actually offers the most hopeful, joyful solution to the problem of man's sin and inability to enter a sinless eternity.

Look at it from this angle: You need someone or something to take the punishment for your sins. Mohammed didn't—never even claimed to. Buddah didn't—wise perhaps but not a savior. L. Ron Hubbard didn't nor did Joseph Smith. Only Jesus died for your sins. Jesus is the only One who claimed to be God and backed up that claim with authentic, verifiable evidence. Jesus is the only One who rose from the grave to give you hope for the future. He's the only One who can make you clean enough to enter heaven.

Jesus didn't just die for the sins of the Western world. He's the sacrifice for the sins of the whole world. He died for the Asians, Middle-Easterners, and Africans, as well as the Europeans, Australians, and North and South Americans. His sacrifice was intended for every man, woman, and child in every country on every continent. He and no other. All roads do not lead to heaven. But thank God there is a road that does—His name is Jesus.

In [Jesus Christ] we have redemption through His blood, the forgiveness of sins, according to the riches of His grace.

EPHESIANS 1:7 NKJV

THE WORLD SAYS:
"Christ is dead."

GOD SAYS:
"The tomb is empty."

God raised him from the dead, freeing him from the agony of death,
because it was impossible for death to keep its hold on him.

ACTS 2:24

You see it more and more these days. Organized groups work to discredit the claims and evidence for the resurrection of Jesus. Secularists, skeptics, and those downright hostile to the gospel rationalize that if Jesus never really rose from the dead, then the whole Christian faith is a sham. Some even go so far as to speculate that He never died in the first place. Beaten, broken, nailed to the cross, pierced with a sword that punctured the lining of His heart, and left hanging for hours unable to get His breath—some detractors actually posit that Jesus was merely unconscious when He was placed in His tomb and later was resuscitated by His friends or regained consciousness on His own. What utter foolishness.

But, what is the evidence for the veracity of the resurrection? What convincing proofs exist to back up the claim that two thousand years ago a man was crucified, buried, and rose again three days later?

Ancient prophesies predicted the resurrection of the Messiah. All four Gospels written by four separate authors agree on the same story, and all four were eyewitnesses to the event. Other witnesses over several days' time, including women, attest to seeing both an empty tomb and the resurrected Christ. If this story were legend, Jewish writers would certainly not have included a woman's testimony.

One of the best arguments lies in the ongoing testimony of the disciples themselves. Even in the face of execution, the early disciples held tight to the belief that Jesus rose from the grave. If they had perpetrated some hoax to advance their cause, it is highly unlikely they would have held on to that lie to the point of death.

Perhaps the greatest evidence of all may be this line from an old and familiar hymn by Alfred H. Ackley: "You ask me how I know He lives—He lives within my heart!"

Blessed be the God and Father of our Lord Jesus Christ, who according to His abundant mercy has begotten us again to a living hope through the resurrection of Jesus Christ from the dead.

1 PETER 1:3 NKJV

THE WORLD SAYS:
"Jesus was a good teacher."

GOD SAYS:
"Jesus is the Son of God."

*We know that the Son of God has come and has given us
understanding so that we may know him who is true;
and we are in him who is true, in his Son Jesus Christ.
He is the true God and eternal life.*

1 JOHN 5:20 NRSV

Which of these statements from Jesus makes Him a good teacher? "You must be born again" (John 3:7). "Blessed are the poor" (Matthew 5:3). "If anyone would come after me, he must deny himself and take up his cross and follow me" (Mark 8:34). Or, "Blessed are you when men hate you" (Luke 6:22). To the biblically literate reader, these lessons are at the very least difficult to understand. To the casual reader, they sound like the opposite of reasonable thinking.

The teachings of Jesus turned the tables on all conventional understanding. He taught about dying to self to get ahead. He talked about His followers eating His flesh and drinking His blood. He talked about many things that could easily be dismissed as complete foolishness. The conclusion would be that He was a crazy teacher rather than a good one—unless you understand the principles hidden just behind His words and acknowledge the mission for which He came to earth in the first place. You simply cannot identify Jesus as a "good teacher" without first identifying Him as the Son of God. It's the only way His teaching makes any sense.

Christ argued with the Pharisees on the merits of His own authority and identity. He probed doubters to see the evidence and believe. Several times, He said things like, "Anyone who has seen me has seen the Father" (John 14:9) and referring to Himself said, "No one has seen the Father except the one who is from God; only he has seen the Father" (John 6:46).

Jesus leaves you with only two options: Write Him off completely as a heretic or receive Him as your Savior and the only begotten Son of God. You must be in the boat or out of the boat. Don't make any assumptions until you've studied the facts.

Who is it that conquers the world but the one who believes that Jesus is the Son of God?

1 JOHN 5:5 NRSV

THE WORLD SAYS:
"Life is short—eat, drink, and be merry."

GOD SAYS:
"Life is eternal—live wisely."

You know that the Lord will reward everyone for whatever good he does.
EPHESIANS 6:8

Is this life all there is? Will we live again after we die? If so, what will that life be like? Everyone must wrestle with these questions, and the answers have serious ramifications for us here and now.

For example, some people believe that this life is all there is. Wise living isn't required "if tomorrow we die," because tomorrow doesn't offer any consequences for our actions today. If this is where you stand, you'd better take a sobering second look. The fact is that if you're right, you have nothing to gain; if you're wrong, you have everything to lose.

And, what if we are eternal creatures as the Bible describes us? What if our eternal future rests on the choices and behaviors we engage in today?

God says we all die and then face judgment. We will approach the throne of God and "God will give to each person according to what he has done" (Romans 2:6). Salvation is a free gift from God that we accept by faith, but our deeds here on earth will determine our rewards in heaven. Wise living yields eternal rewards. But for those who live only for today, there are no rewards at all.

A tale of two destinies. One is darkness; the other, heaven. One will leave you with absolutely nothing but emptiness, sadness, and regret, while the other will leave you well rewarded for your obedience to God's laws and your dedication to carrying out His plans for your life. One is based on what isn't; the other on what is.

Your time here on Earth is but a speck in history. It's hardly noticeable over time—except to God. He knows, He remembers, and He rewards accordingly. Live wisely and make the most of your life for now—and for eternity.

"Behold, I am coming soon! My reward is with me,
and I will give to everyone according to what he has done."
REVELATION 22:12

THE WORLD SAYS:
"Words can't hurt us."

GOD SAYS:
"Life and death are in the power of the tongue."

The tongue has the power of life and death,
and those who love it will eat its fruit.

PROVERBS 18:21

"Sticks and stones can break your bones, but words can never hurt you." Oh, really? Try telling that to the child whose father said, "We never wanted you." Try telling that to the husband whose wife screams, "I hate you." Try telling that to the middle-aged woman who tells herself, "I'm fat and ugly." Words can and do hurt all the time.

Conversely, good words, kind words, and loving words have the opposite effect. Proverbs 25:11 says, "A word aptly spoken is like apples of gold in settings of silver." They are capable of expressing beauty, love, and joy. They can bring peace to a wounded soul. They can restore hope to the hopeless.

Words have power—the power of life and death. They can be used as weapons or as extensions of mercy and compassion, wisdom and understanding, devotion and commitment. Jesus even said that His words are spirit and they are life. (See John 6:63.)

How do your words measure up? Are they loving or hurtful? Jesus says, "I tell you that men will have to give account on the day of judgment for *every* careless word they have spoken. For by your words you will be acquitted, and by your words you will be condemned" (Matthew 12:36–37, emphasis added). Yes. You read it right—every word!

What kind of words do you speak to yourself? Are they words of encouragement and self-esteem? Do your words reflect the fact that God has created you in His own image? If they don't, they should.

Recognizing and appreciating the power of words and using them properly blesses everyone who hears them—including God. "Let the word of Christ dwell in you richly as you teach and admonish one another with all wisdom" (Colossians 3:16). Don't speak down to yourself or others. Remember: Word up!

Pleasant words are a honeycomb,
sweet to the soul and healing to the bones.
PROVERBS 16:24

THE WORLD SAYS:
"No one can know the future."

GOD SAYS:
"Your future is in My hands."

I am convinced that neither death nor life, neither angels nor demons, neither the present nor the future, nor any powers, neither height nor depth, nor anything else in all creation, will be able to separate us from the love of God that is in Christ Jesus our Lord.

ROMANS 8:38–39

The boy tugged on his daddy's pant leg and asked, "Can we go see the fortune-teller?" The father swallowed his circus peanut and looked down, "No, son. Nobody believes in that stuff. No one knows the future." Disappointed, the boy walked on and quietly hoped his father was wrong. The boy wanted certainty in an uncertain world.

Though you do not know what the future holds, you can know who holds the future. Jesus promises to walk with you at all times and in every circumstance. Through wars, illness, stock market crashes, disasters, tests, trials, and other terrible occurrences, God says, "There I'll be, continuing to love you." He also promises to be there during the good times. Either way, you win! He provides love and companionship in good times and bad.

Scripture does tell us some things about the events that will occur in the future. Christ will return. Satan will be thrown into the lake of fire. Believers will receive new heavenly bodies, and they'll enjoy an eternity with God. In other words, great hope resides in those who believe. Consider these words from Jeremiah 29:11 (NRSV): "Surely I know the plans I have for you, says the Lord, plans for your welfare and not for harm, to give you a future with hope."

The future can be a daunting place, filled with mystery and the power of the unknown. But it should not be a scary proposition for the Christian. It should instead be a greater motivation for you to stay close to God, secure in His awareness of what has been, what is, and what will be. It should keep you walking only where He leads and obeying each time He speaks. As you abide in the shadow of the all-knowing One, the future will be secure.

There is surely a future hope for you,
and your hope will not be cut off.
PROVERBS 23:18

THE WORLD SAYS:
"God isn't fair."

GOD SAYS:
"My justice is tempered only by My mercy."

Mercy triumphs over judgment!
JAMES 2:13

Many people enjoy throwing a pity party when troubles come. Raising an angry fist they shout to heaven, "That's not fair, God!"

Well, thank God's goodness and mercy that He isn't fair. If He were, we'd all be sunk. Think about it. We all sin—every one of us. God's Word says sinners deserve condemnation and death. The fair thing is for God to give us eternal punishment starting now. Billy Graham, Mother Teresa, the apostle Paul, and you—all destined for eternal separation from God, if He is fair. But for all our sakes, He isn't.

God actually operates on the other end of the continuum. God says, "You deserve punishment, but I'm going to bless you instead. I'm going to pay the penalty for your disobedience—the debt you cannot pay. As a result, you'll win a prize you didn't earn—salvation." Romans 3:23–24 says it this way: "All have sinned and fall short of the glory of God, and are justified freely by his grace through the redemption that came by Christ Jesus."

Justice demands that we be judged according to the law, which simply points out our own sinfulness. Who has never lied? Or indulged in murderous or lustful thoughts? Under the law, we all stand guilty as charged. But in Christ, there is a new law in operation, the law of the Spirit of life. "Through Christ Jesus the law of the Spirit of life set me free from the law of sin and death" (Romans 8:2).

This is the good news of the gospel. It's the amazing grace of God. Justice is served by Christ taking our sin on the cross, and grace is distributed to all who accept this gift by faith. His pain equals our gain. Thank God for mercy!

Because of the Lord's great love we are not consumed,
for his compassions never fail.

LAMENTATIONS 3:22

THE WORLD SAYS:
"Appearances are everything."

GOD SAYS:
"You look on the outward appearance, but I look on the heart."

Your beauty should not come from outward adornment, such as braided hair and the wearing of gold jewelry and fine clothes. Instead, it should be that of your inner self, the unfading beauty of a gentle and quiet spirit, which is of great worth in God's sight.

1 PETER 3:3–4

Who looks cool to you? For older generations, James Dean represents the epitome of cool. Younger generations might answer Johnny Depp, Audrey Hepburn, Halle Berry, Jude Law, Andre 3000—who have also appeared on best-dressed, cool lists. How about hip-hoppers and rappers with the bling-bling? Many of these musicians excel at braided hair, gold jewelry, and fine clothes. But God says these things do not impress Him. They do not represent real beauty. Looking cool may get you ahead in this world, but true beauty is rewarded by God. It is a beauty that emanates from the inside. It is the beauty of a pure and perfect heart.

The Old Testament prophesies that Jesus had nothing physically attractive about Him that anyone should desire Him. And yet, men, women, and children followed Him throughout the countryside and sat transfixed, hanging on His every word. They were not drawn to His rugged good looks, but rather to the peace that flowed to them from His presence. They were not intrigued by the smooth delivery of His words, but rather by the power of His message. They followed Him not because of His earthly celebrity, but rather to draw healing from His touch.

Inner beauty—the kind that catches the eye of God—cannot be purchased. Even the best plastic surgeon cannot create it. It consists of the virtues of love, joy, and peace—those things that come from encounters with God. It is unaffected by age or genetics.

Are you a beautiful person? Take a good look in the mirror, God's Word. Are you free from the corruption of sin through your relationship with Christ? Is your heart decorated with godly character and loving-kindness? If you don't like what you see, you can do something about it. Inner beauty is the result of extreme exposure to the Son!

The LORD said, "Man looks at the outward appearance, but the LORD looks at the heart."

1 SAMUEL 16:7

THE WORLD SAYS:
"Christians are hypocrites."

GOD SAYS:
"Christians are ordinary people saved by My grace."

Jesus said: "I have not come to call the righteous, but sinners."
MATTHEW 9:13

College students Bill and Hank talked one morning. Hank said, "Are you kidding me? Christians are just a bunch of hypocrites. They talk about love and morality and being a good person, but they're rude, immoral, and judgmental. It doesn't look like following Jesus makes any difference to me."

Hank raises some good questions. If Jesus saves, heals, and redeems people, why don't Jesus' followers reflect more of His character? Why aren't Christians more like Christ? Well, they are—by faith!

But as they exercise their faith and grow in their relationship with God, Christians are just human beings, flawed but forgiven, imperfect but growing in grace. Developing the character of Christ takes time. God calls it "renewing the mind." It wouldn't occur to you to criticize an infant for crying too much or being unable to walk. No one would fault a toddler for bad table manners or finding it difficult to share. You would understand that teenagers are often selfish, obnoxious, and lazy. Christians mature in a similar manner—little by little over time. That's why it's so important that God asks you to be patient and loving with your fellow Christians and, yes, even with yourself.

Salvation itself is a miracle—a transaction that takes place in an instant of time. It transforms a life and translates it from the kingdom of darkness to the kingdom of light. But growing to maturity in God takes time. As some have said, "The Christian walk isn't a sprint. It's a marathon." Growth comes from grace to grace.

The next time you look around at the Christians you know, resist the temptation to point out a failing, a shortcoming, or an act of immaturity. Instead, tell God about it. Ask Him to judge His child as He sees fit, and then ask Him to fill your heart with love and compassion.

Be completely humble and gentle;
be patient, bearing with one another in love.
Ephesians 4:2

THE WORLD SAYS:
"You can't trust anyone."

GOD SAYS:
"You can always trust Me."

"The one who trusts in [Christ] will never be put to shame."
ROMANS 9:33

Who do you trust? Family members are trustworthy—usually. Friends are trustworthy—often. But sooner than later, some or probably all the people in your life will let you down or steer you wrong.

Thankfully, God is more than just another someone. His trustworthiness is flawless, His record perfect. When He makes a promise, He keeps it—no exceptions, no excuses. God is completely true to His Word—and He always has been.

It wasn't God but man who brought untrustworthiness onto the scene. While God was doing exactly what He said He would do, Adam and Eve were doubling back, negotiating the terms, and breaking trust. Their actions got them evicted from the beautiful garden God had created for them, a consequence that God had clearly articulated. How could He be trusted if He had failed to carry through?

Soon after they left Eden, their son also chose the path of broken trust by killing his own brother Abel. It's been a downhill slide ever since. Even the best man or woman cannot be trusted. No wonder God's faithfulness, His trustworthiness, shines so brightly in our lives. We can count on Him—completely and without reservation.

Have you been searching for someone in whom to place your trust? Search no more. God is the One who will never disappoint you, never let you down. You can trust Him with your secrets, your dreams, your broken heart, your future, your life. You can trust Him to keep every single promise He's made to you. You can trust Him for this life and for the life that comes after death. Expect from human beings only what they are capable of giving—a fragmented, well-intentioned trustworthiness at best. Expect from God what only He can give—rock-solid dependability today and forever.

Trust in the Lord with all your heart and lean not on your own understanding; in all your ways acknowledge him, and he will make your paths straight.

Proverbs 3:5–6

THE WORLD SAYS:
"You make your own success."

GOD SAYS:
"Success comes from finding the purpose for which I created you."

I have raised you up for this very purpose, that I might show you my power and that my name might be proclaimed in all the earth.

EXODUS 9:16

Malcolm, an attorney, prided himself on being a self-made man. Born into poverty, he studied hard, graduated valedictorian, and attended Tulane University on a scholarship. Then, he entered Harvard Law School and became junior partner in a well renowned New York City law firm. Soon, he was promoted to senior partner. At one count, he owned six homes. He had yachts, exclusive club memberships, and trophy girlfriends. He thought he had it all, but he lacked one thing: purpose. For all his success, Malcolm felt a deep sense of loneliness and insignificance.

Melinda started life in much the same way Malcolm did. Born into poverty, her mother told her, "God loves you very much, my child. He has a special purpose and plan for your life." As Melinda grew, she discovered an aptitude for law. She also developed a compassion for the poor. Melinda studied hard because she wanted to become a lawyer. Her grades were good enough to win some financial assistance, but she also had to work her way through school. Today, Melinda finds great satisfaction and purpose in being a public defender for those who cannot afford to obtain legal representation. Fighting for the rights of the poor fulfills her lifelong dream, planted in her heart by God. Some days are difficult for Melinda, but every day she takes pride in knowing that she is fulfilling God's special purpose for her life.

Don't be fooled into thinking that success is about acquiring money and prestige. Ask God to help you find the special purpose He has for your life, whether that is to be a corporate lawyer, public defender, street sweeper, union organizer, schoolteacher, or any of the other incalculable number of roles God may have called you to. Find your success in God's will and you will look back only for perspective—never with regret.

We know that all things work together for good for those who love God, who are called according to his purpose.

ROMANS 8:28 NRSV

THE WORLD SAYS:
"All people are the same."

GOD SAYS:
"You are My own unique creation."

You created my inmost being; you knit me together in my mother's womb. I praise you because I am fearfully and wonderfully made; your works are wonderful, I know that full well.

Psalm 139:13–14

The brown-haired baby boy weighed five and one-half pounds at birth. The bald baby was born a full pound heavier. As the weeks turned into months, the smaller baby remained smaller despite a healthy appetite. His features remained finer, sleeker. His thick hair grew thicker. He smiled often yet mainly kept quiet. The larger baby grew heavier still. His bald head produced some hair but it remained thin and sparse. He cried and cooed often but was slow to react to outside stimuli from his parents and caretakers. These twin brothers had vastly different appearances and demeanors.

Every person carries his or her own genetic code. No two people have the same fingerprints, irises in their eyes, or specific facial structures. Even identical twins, who share the same structured code of DNA, develop their own unique personalities and characteristics. The prophet Jeremiah was told by God, "Before I formed you in the womb I knew you, before you were born I set you apart" (Jeremiah 1:5).

It's important for you to recognize and acknowledge your own uniqueness. Until you do, you will not fully understand your own value, and you will miss the opportunity to praise God for His flawless craftsmanship.

When you know that you are God's creation, you will better respect your unique purpose and place in the world. You will understand that your value does not come from your work, your achievements, your lot in life, your connections, or even the good things you do. You will know with certainty that you are precious because God has expended His mighty creative power to make you who you are.

You are the only "you" who has ever been or ever will be—unique in the universe and in God's heart.

When I think of the wisdom and scope of God's plan,
I fall to my knees and pray to the Father, the Creator of everything
in heaven and on earth.
Ephesians 3:14–15 nlt

THE WORLD SAYS:
"Demand your rights."

GOD SAYS:
"If someone takes your coat, offer him your shirt also."

If your enemy is hungry, give him food to eat; if he is thirsty, give him water to drink. In doing this, you will heap burning coals on his head, and the LORD will reward you.

PROVERBS 25:21–22

A wife demands that her husband help her with the household chores. A husband tells his wife that if she loves him, she will be willing to do things his way. A woman demands credit for an idea her boss presented to management. A man demands a raise and promotion he feels he's earned. A woman demands an apology from a friend before she will forgive a perceived wrong. A man insists that his neighbor answer for the damage done to his lawn by his neighbor's pet. People are always looking to get what they have coming.

Implicitly and explicitly, the Bible takes a different tack. It encourages us to give up our rights for Christ's sake and focus instead on serving others. Jesus himself urged His followers to give in order to receive, to put themselves last if they wish to be first, to lose their lives if they wish to find them.

It almost seems counterintuitive to give up your rights. It feels like you're losing a part of yourself. But God's ways are often contrary to the ways that seem right to your human nature. God isn't asking you to follow blindly, though. He has proven that His ways are higher and better than our own. Your way might get you that raise you've been promised, but doing things God's way might bring about opportunities you've never even dreamed of.

Turn the tables on the circumstances in your life by praying for those who treat you badly, giving to those who withhold from you, loving those who have not been loving to you. Demanding what you are owed is a shortsighted approach that will rob you of lasting satisfaction. Surrendering your rights to God will give you more than you deserve. It will give you the riches of God's love and grace poured out on your behalf.

Those who love their life in this world will lose it. Those who despise their life in this world will keep it for eternal life.

JOHN 12:25 NLT

THE WORLD SAYS:
"Get all you can."

GOD SAYS:
"Give all you can."

*Jesus said, "Give, and it will be given to you.
A good measure, pressed down, shaken together and
running over, will be poured into your lap."*

LUKE 6:38

Remember the story in the old movie *It's a Wonderful Life*? George Bailey, played by Jimmy Stewart, lives a selfless life, giving time and treasure while working down at the old Building and Loan. He forsakes college and even his own honeymoon to help his friends and neighbors of Bedford Falls. Out of his own pocket, he keeps the citizens afloat during a particularly bad economic downturn. One Christmas Eve, George misplaces $8,000 and becomes extremely depressed. Mean old Mr. Potter almost ruins George, but at the last minute, the people of Bedford Falls rally together and pay back the lost $8,000. George rejoices when he sees the promise of a lifetime of giving.

You can't outgive God. If you live to give, God will continue to give to you. If you live to get, you might have short-term gain, but you'll lose out in the end.

Mean Mr. Potter wanted to get all he could. He tried to buy up Bedford Falls and even buy out George Bailey, but he couldn't do it. For all his greed, Mr. Potter only got more and more cantankerous, callow, and hardened. In gaining the world, he lost his soul.

The premise of this old movie comes straight out of the Bible. When you give, you not only bless others, you bless yourself. You realize that all blessings are from God. You see firsthand the love of God visited upon others. You see joy and happiness come to others. You see them praise their Father in heaven. This, in turn, yields its own pleasures. And, like George Bailey, you might see others have an opportunity to give to you in your hour of need. The cycle of giving feeds itself, while the cycle of getting and taking eventually wears itself out. Think about it this way: Give and receive, or get and receive not. It's your choice.

Each of you must give as you have made up your mind, not reluctantly or under compulsion, for God loves a cheerful giver.

2 Corinthians 9:7 NRSV

THE WORLD SAYS:
"God is unknowable."

GOD SAYS:
"I have revealed Myself to you through My Son, Jesus Christ."

Jesus said: "I and the Father are one."
JOHN 10:30

They liked the same things, dressed the same, acted the same, and told the same silly jokes. They called the son "a chip off the old block." They had the same occupation and even had the same name. Though they lived hundreds of miles apart, if you knew one, you knew the other. In fact, they even looked the same. People would sometimes mistake the father for the son when looking at old photographs. When the son phoned, people would think it was the father. Except for their age, they were indistinguishable.

Who doesn't know "a chip off the old block"? Who doesn't know a son who is just like his father? Jesus is just like His Heavenly Father. In fact, their similarities go beyond what mere earthly fathers and sons share. Jesus is an exact representation of God in human form. He is God in the flesh. The Bible calls Him "God incarnate."

If Jesus equals God, then we can look to Jesus to find out about God's character and concerns. Jesus fed the poor, healed the sick, taught the multitudes, rebuked the unrighteous, and paid the price for our sins. He was filled with compassion and kindness, justice and mercy. Jesus lived a sinless life, always told the truth, always lived the truth, and always acted in love—absolutely always.

The ancient Romans erected a statue that said, "To an unknown God." Some religions today pride themselves on the mystery of God. Still others have forsaken even the idea of a personal god and worship a force or presence. Only Christianity claims to have a God who dwelt among and walked with them. Christians worship a God who can be known. If you know Jesus, you know the Father. They're one and the same.

In [Christ] dwells all the fullness of the Godhead bodily.
Colossians 2:9 nkjv

THE WORLD SAYS:
"It's just a little white lie."

GOD SAYS:
"He who guards his lips guards his life."

Whoever guards his mouth and tongue keeps his soul from troubles.
PROVERBS 21:23 NKJV

"Billy, did you spill the milk?"

"No, Mommy. The kitty-cat did it." Nine-year-old Billy told his mother a lie. He had been hasty in putting food back into the refrigerator and knocked over the milk. He thought it didn't really matter, but when his mother discovered the truth, he lost a lot more than he expected.

The ninth commandment states, "You shall not give false testimony against your neighbor" (Exodus 20:16). In other words, "Do not lie." You might make a distinction between big lies and little white lies, but God doesn't. He just says, "Don't do it." He leaves no wiggle room. He makes no provision for exceptions.

This makes it difficult when situations say it would be much easier to lie than to tell the truth. But God says lying is a very big deal because lies—no matter how big or small—have consequences.

First, lies erode trust. When you catch someone in a lie, even a little white one, you wonder what other lies the speaker has told. You might wonder if *anything* that person tells you is trustworthy or true. Just like that, there is a breach of confidence and credibility.

Second, lies anger God. God says He hates lying lips. And this response seems to be across the board. He does not follow up this statement with caveats like "unless you're just trying to spare someone's feelings" or "unless the lie is inconsequential."

The person who first said, "Honesty is the best policy," was wise indeed. Lying is always a bad idea, and the truth is always the way to go. In a situation where you find yourself caught between the truth and a hard place, silence is your next best option. Lying complicates and inflames everything it touches.

Fasten the belt of truth around your waist, and put on the breastplate of righteousness.
Ephesians 6:14 nrsv

THE WORLD SAYS:
"Prayer is an empty exercise."

GOD SAYS:
"Prayer changes everything."

Jesus said, "Whatever you ask for in prayer, believe that you have received it, and it will be yours."

Mark 11:24

Marty's doctor gave him the bad news. Marty had a rare arterial disease and would need radical surgery. The surgery would be risky and might even result in death, but without it, Marty would likely have a heart attack or stroke and a premature death. Devastated, Marty realized the only way to make it through this ordeal would be to pray.

That's what makes prayer so powerful. It's an option that trumps all other judgments. It's an opportunity to plead your case to a higher court—the court of God. Wholehearted devotees, marginal believers, even unbelievers have been known to grasp at this last best chance in time of crisis.

Many who have taken their case to God in prayer have had their sentences reversed and their lives changed. But even those in whose situation God chooses not to intervene would probably say that the exercise was meaningful. It offered them a sense of peace and acceptance, comfort and guidance to deal with their adverse circumstances. Even though their situation did not change, their approach to it, and often their perspective about it, did.

No matter what the outcome, prayer always changes the one who prays. It forces the person praying to step out from behind their homebound thoughts and reach out to God. The simplest prayer not only presumes the existence of God and the possibility of relationship with Him, but it also activates God's involvement on behalf of the person praying and those he is praying for.

If you have a need in your life, don't hesitate to lift your voice in prayer to God. Pour out your heart to the one Person who holds the key to the future. You can be sure that the One who sees all and knows all will act in your ultimate best interest. But expect to walk away a changed person. Prayer changes everything and everyone—even you!

Jesus said, "You will call upon me and come and pray to me, and I will listen to you."
JEREMIAH 29:12

THE WORLD SAYS:
"You are who you are."

GOD SAYS:
"You are who I created you to be."

God said, "Let us make man in our image, in our likeness…"
GENESIS 1:26

In the late 1980s, Grant commanded attention as a notorious drag queen. He defined life on his own terms and had a small following. But when lovers couldn't satisfy his spiritual needs and friends started dying from AIDS, he began to question his identity. Then the doctor said, "Grant, I'm sorry, but you're HIV positive." This news rocked him to his core. He questioned who he was and reexplored his Christian roots.

To his amazement, Grant discovered that God loved him—something he had believed was not the case—and he reached out for a relationship with Him. In the months ahead, Grant found sexual healing and wholeness.

After giving his life to Christ in 1993, Grant no longer practiced the homosexual/drag queen lifestyle. With God's help, he remained celibate, and in 1998 Grant married Patrice, a former practicing lesbian. Today, Grant and Patrice work together and counsel others who wish to escape the homosexual lifestyle and choose to live in Christ, taking on His identity rather than their own flawed, former selves.

Like Grant and Patrice, you were created by God for His purposes. You might not have lived a homosexual lifestyle, but you might have been like a stubborn sheep, wandering off to go your own way. You were not created for sin. You were not created to define your own lifestyle and identity. Those who live their lives their own way may find temporary rewards, but ultimately it's a sham, a counterfeit, a lie.

God created you to enjoy fellowship with Him and others, on His terms, not yours. He created you with certain gifts, talents, aptitudes, and personality traits that were designed for His glory. You were created by God in His image with free will and the capacity to love, respond, interact, and make choices. Discover the you that God created you to be, and live it to the fullest for His glory.

Jesus said, "I am the light of the world. Whoever follows me will never walk in darkness, but will have the light of life."

John 8:12

THE WORLD SAYS:
"You were born this way."

GOD SAYS:
"You can be born again."

You have been born again, not of perishable seed, but of imperishable, through the living and enduring word of God.

1 PETER 1:23

The lyrics to a Christian worship song read, "I'm a new creation. I'm a brand-new man. Old things are passed away. I am born again." These words remind the singer that they no longer have a sin nature, but a new spirit. They also encourage the unbeliever to place their faith in a life-changing God. God says that not only can you change, but you must change.

Jesus said, "I tell you the truth, no one can see the kingdom of God unless he is born again" (John 3:3). Being born again is both a blessing and a requirement. It's a blessing because it offers its recipients a fresh start. In the Bible, God tells us to forget about how we were or who we are. Everything has been changed by His presence in our lives. We have become new people.

Being "born again" is a requirement because Jesus says it is necessary for entry into the kingdom of God. God and sin cannot coexist. If you are going to enter a new life in Christ, your dead sin nature needs to be removed and replaced with something alive. So, upon receiving Christ into your life as your Lord and Savior, God takes away your sin and gives you a new, live spirit. Through this supernatural act, you become "born again."

Do you struggle with lying, lust, anger, or violence? You can become a whole different person—you can be born again. Do you have a problem with addiction, feelings of worthlessness, or laziness and procrastination? Don't despair. All those things can be swept away when God comes into your life—you can be born again to a new life. Don't continue to languish. Let God get rid of the old and bring in the new. It's not who you are that matters; it's who you can be.

If anyone is in Christ, he is a new creation;
the old has gone, the new has come!

2 CORINTHIANS 5:17

THE WORLD SAYS:
"We can't change the past."

GOD SAYS:
"You can use the past to change your future."

Be made new in the attitude of your minds.
EPHESIANS 4:23

How great is it that God uses flawed people? If He didn't, we'd all be sunk. Every single one of us has junk in our past. Most likely, we'd rather sweep these past sins and indiscretions under a rug, but God wants us to bring them into the light. In the light of God, our past can be used as a testimony of His goodness.

Every single negative act or character flaw on the planet is merely a testimony waiting to happen. Here's the script: "I used to be like this, but God changed me." The words *but God* mean He does a work that changes a negative past into a positive future. They mean He can do the same thing for someone else that He did for you. They mean God still moves in the lives of people today.

People need authenticity. They need to see people like themselves, warts and all, so that they can see how far God's love and forgiveness reach. If you cover up your past, then the grace of God in your life is hidden—God can't use it to touch the life of someone else.

The apostle Paul was quick to disclose his past—and even quicker to declare the remedy. He told everyone he met that he was the greatest of all sinners, that he had persecuted and killed Christians. He took no pleasure in discussing the past but used it as a means to contrast his past acts with his present. In order to demonstrate that he was a changed man, Paul had to reveal from what he had been changed. He uncovered the past in order to glory in the transforming power of God.

You can't change the past, but you can use it to change the future in your life and the lives of others.

If we confess our sins, he is faithful and just and will forgive us our sins and purify us from all unrighteousness.

1 JOHN 1:9

THE WORLD SAYS:
"The devil is just a myth."

GOD SAYS:
"Your enemy, the devil, prowls around like a roaring lion, seeking to devour you."

Be self-controlled and alert. Your enemy the devil prowls around like a roaring lion looking for someone to devour.

1 PETER 5:8

It's easy to believe in evil. Just look around the world. Wars, tyrants, murders, rapes, and many other injustices abound. Even natural disasters create their havoc. But an actual personification of evil called the devil? C'mon, that's just a myth, isn't it?

The Bible is clear in its declaration that such a being actually exists. The story is that the rebellious angel Satan fell from heaven and took a third of the angels with him. They are now called demons. Satan tempted Adam and Eve to sin. Since then, Satan and his demons have continued to torment, tempt, and devour humankind in an effort to defeat God's purposes on earth.

Make no mistake about it. Satan not only exists, but he's out to get you if you are walking in relationship with God. He will go to extraordinary lengths to steal, kill, and destroy everything good in your life—if you let him.

God has given us two effective weapons to use against the "adversary of our souls"—scripture and prayer.

Jesus defended Himself against the devil by quoting God's own words: "The Devil took [Jesus] to the peak of a very high mountain and showed him the nations of the world and all their glory, 'I will give it all to you,' he said, 'if you will only kneel down and worship me.' 'Get out of here, Satan,' Jesus told him. For the Scriptures say, 'You must worship the Lord your God; serve only Him'" (Matthew 4:8–10 NLT).

Jesus later told His disciples: "Watch and pray, lest you enter into temptation. The spirit indeed is willing, but the flesh is weak" (Matthew 26:41 NKJV).

There's a full-blown battle to the death going on for your soul. Don't be lulled into a false sense of security by those who would tell you the devil is a figment of human imagination. He's your very real, sworn enemy.

Put on the whole armor of God, that you may be able to stand against the wiles of the devil.

EPHESIANS 6:11 NKJV

THE WORLD SAYS:
"Religion is a crutch."

GOD SAYS:
"Living faith energizes and restores."

Be very careful to act exactly as God commands you. Don't veer off to the right or the left. Walk straight down the road God commands so that you'll have a good life.

DEUTERONOMY 5:32–33 MSG

TRUTH.

The question is not whether religion is a crutch—it clearly is—but rather what kind of crutch you are leaning on. Can it support your weight in the hard times? Can it help you get from where you are to where you need to be? Can it facilitate healing and recovery?

No one lives in a vacuum. Everyone has a religion of some kind. Many people worship at the throne of money, power, drugs, sex, beauty, emotional highs, physical strength, and any number of other temporal persuasions. They lean on them expectantly, hoping to find fulfillment, happiness, satisfaction, peace. But they've put their weight on a crutch that is structurally unsound. Sooner rather than later, they will find themselves bruised and broken on the floor.

Christianity is a different type of religion. Is it a crutch? Of course! The Bible is filled with God's encouragement to lean on Him, trust Him, put your cares on Him, depend on Him. It's a crutch with substance and strength enough to carry you through every difficulty this life might bring. It's a crutch designed and built by the Creator of the universe Himself—completely dependable, custom-made just for you.

And your Christian faith will do more than just hold you up. It will also energize and restore you, allowing you to walk worthy of the unique purpose and calling for which you were created. In fact, it has the power to lead you straight into the presence of God Almighty.

We all need a crutch to get us through this life. It's mighty important which crutch you choose to lean on, however. Go with the one that has been tried and proven through time and eternity past. Only then can you be sure it will hold you up now and throughout your eternal future.

Be very careful, then, how you live—not as unwise but as wise.
Ephesians 5:15

THE WORLD SAYS:
"You have the right to be free."

GOD SAYS:
"You are free to do what's right."

You…were called to be free. But do not use your freedom to indulge the sinful nature; rather, serve one another in love.

GALATIANS 5:13

Remember the hippies of the 1960s? They insisted on "free love." They said, "If you can't be with the one you love, then love the one you are with." In other words, they endorsed having sex with whomever, whenever. Many of the hippies also promoted casual drug use. To them, "freedom," "peace," and "love" weren't just slogans; they were commands to live a life of hedonism.

God offers a different kind of freedom. He loves to set people free from sin and addiction. He loves to make people whole. He longs to see people operating out of His strength. He knows that His freedom is true liberation. "If the Son sets you free, you will be free indeed" (John 8:36). What great news!

The freedom of Christ is not a wanton, licentious freedom to indulge in whatever you want. It's actually freedom not to sin. It's a freedom to live for God. The Bible says, "You have been set free from sin and have become slaves to righteousness" (Romans 6:18). In other words, your freedom in Christ transfers you from bondage to holiness. You are now bound to live rightly.

Surely you remember what it was like before you met Christ. You wanted to do the right things, but somehow they always seemed to elude you. Your best intentions ended up stinking of selfishness and personal gratification. That kind of freedom is no freedom at all. You are free only when you are able to choose your course and follow it through to completion. That comes only through relationship with Christ.

Freedom in Christ affords you the freedom to love others, worship God, walk in integrity, grow in grace and the character of God—all fruitful pursuits that produce eternal benefits. Don't waste your freedom—use it to live for God.

Live as free men, but do not use your freedom as a cover-up for evil; live as servants of God.

1 PETER 2:16

THE WORLD SAYS:
"Good guys finish last."

GOD SAYS:
"Good guys finish first."

Sitting down, Jesus called the Twelve and said, "If anyone wants to be first, he must be the very last, and the servant of all."

MARK 9:35

"Congratulations, honey. I knew you could do it." That's what the father wanted to say to his figure-skating daughter on the day of the championships. Instead, he saw her fall not once but three times during her routine. She ended up dead last out of twenty competitors. What would he tell his daughter now?

Nobody likes to lose, let alone wind up in last place. The world will tell you that if you spend your time doing good and trying to please God, nobody will be happy for you. In fact, many people shake their heads and think bright Christians are wasting their talents and minds if they don't jump onto the fast track of success. To this issue, Jesus says the unexpected. Jesus says winners live a life of selfless service.

Serve the poor. Serve children. Serve the helpless. Serve those who can't serve themselves. These are the earmarks of greatness. James 1:27 says, "Religion that God our Father accepts as pure and faultless is this: to look after orphans and widows in their distress...." Opportunities for service abound.

And what about the father and his figure-skating daughter? He was unprepared for what he saw. Instead of seeing his daughter completely undone by her failure, he saw her congratulate the winner. He also saw her pick up skates and other gear and take them back into the locker room. He saw her serve her teammates and the sport in general. Come time for the award ceremony, she received a special merit of achievement for greatness of character. Later she told her dad that that award meant more to her than any award she could have earned out on the ice.

Our little figure skater demonstrates the principle taught by Jesus more than two thousand years ago. It is possible to come in last and still finish first.

"My kingdom," said Jesus, "doesn't consist of
what you see around you."
JOHN 18:36 MSG

TRUTH.

THE WORLD SAYS:
"No one will know."

GOD SAYS:
"I see all things."

He rules forever by his power, his eyes watch the nations—
let not the rebellious rise up against him.

PSALM 66:7

Who hasn't been freaked out by the lyrics to this Christmas song? "He sees you when you're sleeping. He knows when you're awake. He knows if you've been bad or good, so be good for goodness sake." Having good ole Saint Nick watching you at all times almost seems like some B-level horror movie. It's creepy. We Americans value our privacy. We want the freedom to do things that "no one will ever know."

Unlike Saint Nick, God really does see all and know all. The Bible tells us that "even the very hairs of your head are all numbered" (Matthew 10:30). He sees when every sparrow falls (see verse 29). He knows your every need because He sees your every circumstance. Nothing you do escapes His gaze.

Now, this would be creepy and scary if God wasn't completely good. If God was unjust, He could exploit your flaws and sins to humiliate or embarrass you or cause your ruin. But He has no mean streak, and He uses His knowledge of your greatest secrets for your eternal good.

How can He do that, you might ask? Well, if He sees you in need, He can meet your need. If He sees that you have sinned (and He sees everyone's missteps—everyone), He can make a way out of it so that you don't have to face punishment for it. (Remember, He is good and wants nobody to perish.) On Judgment Day, God will expose our every deed, good and bad. If we have accepted Christ as our Lord and Savior, our misdeeds will be deferred to the crucified Christ, who died on our behalf. If we have not accepted Christ, our exposed sins will die with us as we face eternal separation from God.

God sees your every move. It's both a terror and a comfort. Thank God He is altogether good.

The LORD watches over the way of the righteous.

PSALM 1:6

THE WORLD SAYS:
"Don't ever let go."

GOD SAYS:
"Relinquish control."

Jesus said, "Remember Lot's wife!"
LUKE 17:32

Lot and his family lived in Sodom, a city of rampant sin. God planned to destroy Sodom, but He was pleased with Lot so He sent an angel to Lot to tell him to get out. The angels led Lot's family to the edge of town and told them, "Flee for your lives! Don't look back, and don't stop anywhere on the plain." Lot's family started running and God began to rain fire down on Sodom. But as they traveled, Lot's wife got anxious. She wanted to see what was happening behind her. Eventually, she couldn't help herself any longer. She looked back and turned into a pillar of salt! (See Genesis 19:15–26.)

A pillar of salt? C'mon! It's not like she lied or killed somebody. She looked back. Where's the crime in that? Why would God punish her so harshly?

Lot's wife committed the crime of trying to hold on to her old life. She second-guessed God's best for her, and she wanted to return to the old life she had left behind. In the process, she forfeited the deliverance and salvation God had provided for her.

Many people strive to retain the things they think they so desperately need. They say, "I need this house, this car, this girlfriend, this lifestyle." They hold on to these things so tightly, their fingers cramp and lose blood. They become frozen. God wants to give you things that really matter. We aren't talking about divine punishment; we're talking about simple physics: You can't take hold of the new until you've let go of the old. The Bible puts it this way: "Those who cling to worthless idols forfeit the grace that could be theirs" (Jonah 2:8).

When you hold on to things you think you desperately need, God can't give you His better option. Why turn yourself into a pillar of salt? Why not receive the very best from Him?

Jesus said, "Whoever tries to keep his life will lose it, and whoever loses his life will preserve it."

Luke 17:33

THE WORLD SAYS:
"You're too old to change."

GOD SAYS:
"You're never too old to become the person you were created to be."

There is a future hope for you, and your hope will not be cut off.
PROVERBS 24:14

What do the movies *Space Cowboys, On Golden Pond, Cocoon,* and *Marty* all have in common? These movies all feature stories of great achievement by people considered to be past their prime.

When Abraham was old, God told him that he was going to have a son who would father a whole nation called Israel. Abraham was amused and waited, but no son came. Abraham's wife, Sarah, said to Abraham, "You've got to do something about this."

Sarah presented her plan. Abraham would sleep with her handmaiden, Hagar, and have a son with her. In this way, they would acquire an heir and help God fulfill His promise.

Eighty-one-year-old Abraham went along with Sarah's plan and slept with Hagar. As a result, a son named Ishmael was born. But far from fulfilling God's plan, they only brought trouble into their lives. God had something even more remarkable in store for the elderly couple. Nineteen years later, at one hundred years of age, Abraham fathered a son through his wife, Sarah. They were so amused and overjoyed that they named their son Isaac, which means "laughter."

Like Sarah and Abraham, lots of people panic because they think they are growing too old to see God's promise, His blessing, His purpose in their lives. They are often tempted to strike out on their own and try to move things along—always with disastrous results.

God doesn't want or need your help. What He does want and need is your patience, your endurance, your faithfulness. Don't ever believe the lie that you are too old to be used by God. He is not limited by time or age or anything else, and He will not pass you by. Hang in there. God's promises are absolute.

Those who are planted in the house of the LORD shall flourish in the courts of our God. They shall still bear fruit in old age; they shall be fresh and flourishing.

PSALM 92:13–14 NKJV

THE WORLD SAYS:
"You have to bend the rules to get ahead."

GOD SAYS:
"Nothing good will be withheld from those who walk in integrity."

The man of integrity walks securely, but he who takes crooked paths will be found out.

PROVERBS 10:9

How do those who have it all, get it all? Are all prosperous men liars and cheaters? Is it possible to get ahead and still walk in integrity? The story of Job addresses these questions in a fascinating way.

Job of the Old Testament did have it all—a wife, large family, large herds of animals, many servants, and a nice house. He also lived a blameless and upright life, fearing God and shunning evil. He did no wrong, and God blessed him. One day, everything changed. All his animals were stolen. All his servants were killed. All his children died in an accident. Adding insult to injury, painful sores covered Job from the soles of his feet to the top of his head.

Lacking faith, Job's wife realized God must have abandoned her husband. She told Job, "Curse God and die!" (Job 2:9). At that point, she didn't see the value in following God. God seemed to be punishing them for no good reason. Rebellion, cheating, lying, and bending the rules seemed like a fair option to her at that time.

If you were Job, what would you do? Would you curse God and die? Would you say to yourself, "I guess I was a fool to serve God. Next time, I'll scratch my way to the top any way I can"? Or would you say like Job did, "The Lord gave and the Lord has taken away; may the name of the Lord be praised" (Job 1:21)?

Since Job remained faithful and walked uprightly, the second half of his life was even better than the first. "The LORD made [Job] prosperous again and gave him twice as much as he had before" (Job 42:10). Endure in goodness and faithfulness—even if calamity strikes—and see how God rewards your faithfulness and integrity.

See, the Sovereign LORD comes with power, and his arm rules for him. See, his reward is with him, and his recompense accompanies him.

ISAIAH 40:10

THE WORLD SAYS:
"You'll never amount to anything."

GOD SAYS:
"I have a plan for your life— a plan to give you hope and a future."

It's in Christ that we find out who we are and what we are living for. Long before we first heard of Christ and got our hopes up, he had his eye on us, had designs on us for glorious living, part of the overall purpose he is working out in everything and everyone.

EPHESIANS 1:11–12 MSG

Nobody thought he would survive. He looked like a monster—just a little mass of burned flesh. After a terrible accident in the family car, Joel sustained burns over 85 percent of his body. Remarkably, he lived. As he grew, Joel endured many painful surgeries and hospitalizations. His skin had to be surgically cut to allow for growth. Everyone feared he would turn out socially and mentally stunted. Throughout the ordeal, Joel's parents loved him and encouraged him.

Today, Joel is a nationally known motivational speaker. His other achievements are extensive. He was student body president, an Eagle Scout, captain of his soccer team, Olympic torchbearer, and Citizen of the Year. He has been praised by governors, senators, and presidents. He has appeared on many television news magazine programs and tried acting. Newspapers and magazines across the country have covered his story. He's even written an autobiography called *Joel*. Throughout it all, he has maintained an upbeat attitude of joy and thankfulness. He has touched the lives of thousands, if not millions. Out of the ashes, God has given Joel a hope and a future.

Joel had good reason to believe that he had no future and God didn't care. He could have believed that he would never amount to anything. But he refused to give in to stinking thinking. Joel beat the odds—not only did he live but he also became a successful man despite his injuries. He still lives life full of hope and happiness.

No matter what anybody has told you, no matter how injured you are, no matter how sick you are, no matter how rich or poor you are, God can bless you and use your life. We all have a role to play in God's kingdom. Don't let anybody anytime tell you otherwise. Keep hope alive!

The plans of the Lord stand firm forever,
the purposes of his heart through all generations.

Psalm 33:11

THE WORLD SAYS:
"If you don't stand up for yourself, no one else will."

GOD SAYS:
"I will contend with those who contend with you."

This is what the Lord says: "Yes, captives will be taken from warriors, and plunder retrieved from the fierce; I will contend with those who contend with you, and your children I will save."

ISAIAH 49:25

They called him "Billy the Bully"—the meanest kid in the seventh grade. At five foot eight, he loved to beat up Maurice, a small, nervous kid who liked to play chess. Then thirteen-year-old Johnny moved into town. At a full six feet tall, Johnny's height drew immediate attention. This attention made him feel awkward and shy. Hence, he felt a natural affinity for the equally socially challenged Maurice. Today, they are inseparable best of friends, and "Billy the Bully" bothers Maurice no more.

Who sticks up for you? Who is watching your back? The government means well, but it doesn't always come through. Good defense attorneys charge too much. Family members and friends may walk out on you. Employers may let you go for financial reasons. Only God can be trusted to look out for your best interests. God is your body-and-soul guard. He has promised to contend with those who contend with you—no exceptions, no excuses. When you need Him, He's there.

How can you know that this is true, that God will never leave you or forsake you? Consider this: Didn't God hurl Israel's Egyptian oppressors into the Red Sea? Didn't God send David to kill Israel's enemy Goliath? Didn't God save the three Hebrew children from death when they were thrown into the fiery furnace? Furthermore, didn't God instead punish their would-be killers?

God punished sin by allowing Jesus to die upon the cross. And God triumphed over evil by raising Jesus from the dead. God will ultimately contend with Satan by binding him up and throwing him into a lake of fire. God is always watching your back. Trust in Him and His love and provision and see what He does. No matter what may come, nothing can separate you from God's love.

"The LORD your God is with you, he is mighty to save.
He will take great delight in you, he will quiet you with his love,
he will rejoice over you with singing."

ZEPHANIAH 3:17

THE WORLD SAYS:
"There is a higher power."

GOD SAYS:
"I am the highest power."

*"I am the Alpha and the Omega, the First and the Last,
the Beginning and the End."*

REVELATION 22:13

Moses trembled. God himself was speaking to him from a burning bush. God told Moses, "I am sending you to Pharaoh to bring my people...out of Egypt" (Exodus 3:10). Moses wanted verification from God. Convincing the Israelites that their God wanted them to pack up and leave would be very difficult. Nothing less than a power and authority greater than Pharaoh would convince them that they were to go. So, Moses asked God, "What is your name? What should I tell the Israelites?" God said to Moses, "I am who I am. This is what you are to say to the Israelites: I AM has sent me to you" (verse 14).

Some might say God is being a little vague here. Why would the ultimate authority and power in the universe call Himself I AM? Wouldn't something like "Master of the Universe" be better? I AM implies ultimate reality. I AM implies eternal existence. I AM means before anything else existed on the planet, God was. I AM means He'll always be here, too. I AM means everything else is temporary or created and therefore subject to the ultimate authority of I AM. I AM means God is the highest power in heaven or earth.

If the great I AM isn't the highest power, then other powers can claim that position. Love, "the force," Buddah, Krishna, "something out there," and Mother Earth have all been claimed by some people as a form of higher power. But all they have is a claim—with no evidence to back it up.

Meanwhile, Pharaoh eventually released the Israelites with the power of the great I AM. God's people then entered the Promised Land. One of the greatest things about I AM is that I AM wants to know you intimately and live in and through you. How will you respond?

There is none like you, O Lord; you are great,
and your name is great in might.
JEREMIAH 10:6 NRSV

THE WORLD SAYS:
"A loving God wouldn't allow all this suffering."

GOD SAYS:
"I created a perfect world. Suffering is a product of sin."

I consider that the sufferings of this present time are not worth comparing with the glory about to be revealed to us.

ROMANS 8:18 NRSV

Life stinks. Wars, sickness, plagues, floods, and terrorist attacks assail the world every day. Why would a good God allow such suffering? Without an adequate answer, many choose not to place their faith in a loving God. For some, human suffering discourages faith.

A deeper question might be, "Why is there suffering at all?" If this question can be answered, faith in a good God might be possible.

The problem of suffering all starts with sin. Sin first reared its ugly head when Satan rebelled from God and took a third of the angels with him. When God created a perfect world with two perfect people, Satan came along and tempted Adam and Eve to sin. The mother and father of us all ate forbidden fruit. In doing so, they passed down a sin condition all humans inherit. Everyone sins, and the very sin creates suffering.

What about natural disasters, diseases, and other things beyond human control? Did the sin of Adam and Eve start that type of suffering, too? Unfortunately the answer to that question is also yes. Scripture says, "The whole creation has been groaning as in the pains of childbirth right up to the present time" (Romans 8:22). Adam and Eve's sin started death, decay, and destruction for nature, also—it all came in the wake of human sin and rebellion against God.

Therefore, all suffering results from sin, starting with Adam and Eve and continuing on to our own. But God remains good. He gave humans the freedom to obey Him or not. When humans chose not to obey, they brought on sin and suffering. It's not a pleasant thought. It's hard to accept for some. But it's the truth. Thank God that someday He'll remove all sin and suffering and restore peace and order to the universe. God will eventually clean up the mess. Meanwhile, let's place our faith and trust in Him.

Jesus said "In this world you will have trouble. But take heart! I have overcome the world."

JOHN 16:33

THE WORLD SAYS:
"Life is the result of evolution."

GOD SAYS:
"In the beginning, I created the heavens and the earth."

In the beginning God created the heavens and the earth.
GENESIS 1:1 NKJV

In his book *The Origin of Species*, Charles Darwin postulates a theory that revolutionized the scientific community and the world. He wrote about "natural selection," a process called evolution where organisms survive by adapting and changing over time. Evolutionary theory then developed to explain all life forms in mere scientific terms. Life forms morphed from organic matter to one-celled organisms to more complex organisms. And, by implication, mankind (or *Homo sapiens*) came from hominids (or monkeys). But can this theory agree with what the Bible says?

The Bible claims God created the heavens and earth in six days. During these days, He uniquely created each species. Then at the end of the six days, God made man in His own image and breathed the breath of life into him.

If evolution is true, why would God be necessary? If God is not necessary, then we owe Him nothing. He becomes irrelevant. At best, He becomes a passive bystander while the earth evolved. In fact, if evolution were true, God needn't have been there at all. That's why this debate is so significant. It's much more than a scientific debate. It explains fundamentally who we are.

Today, serious doubt has fallen on Darwinism. Scientists of like mind have banded together and raised issue with the icons of evolutionary theory. These include the Stanley Miller experiment of the "primordial soup," Darwin's "Tree of Life," Haeckel's embryo argument, which claims the similarity of embryos among different species, and the "Missing Links" fossil record.

These award-winning scientists view the complexity of heaven and earth and see support for the existence of God, not the absence of God. If brilliant scientists and scholars can see God's design in the earth and its inhabitants, why can't you?

> *In the beginning was the Word, and the Word*
> *was with God, and the Word was God. He was*
> *in the beginning with God. All things were*
> *made through Him, and without Him*
> *nothing was made that was made.*
> John 1:1–3 NKJV

TRUTH.

THE WORLD SAYS:
"Do unto others before they can do unto you."

GOD SAYS:
"Do unto others as you want them to do unto you."

Jesus said: "Love your neighbor as yourself."
MARK 12:31

Jesus taught the Golden Rule to His followers gathered on the Galilean hillside. Like many of His other teachings, this one turned the tables on the natural bent of men and women. Assuming that all human beings are out for themselves, they pursue security by taking an aggressive, first-strike stance. Get the other guy before he gets you.

On the surface, this philosophy seems reasonable. Why sit around waiting to be wronged? Assume it's going to happen sooner or later and take action. A good offense is the best defense. Delve a little deeper, however, and you will easily see that such a mind-set enforces a cycle of aggression—a cycle of hurt and retribution that results in a lose-lose situation for everyone.

Jesus proposed a different approach. Treat others not as you expect that they'll treat you—badly; but treat them as you'd like to be treated—kindly, fairly, lovingly. If practiced, this way of thinking effectively stops the cycle of negative aggression in its tracks before sending it flying off in the opposite direction. All it takes is one enlightened soul to literally reformulate society. Suddenly, lose-lose becomes win-win.

This important principle can make your world a better place to live if you're willing to let God help you rigorously practice it. What a wonderful opportunity—a one-person social revolution.

Jesus first taught the Golden Rule more than two thousand years ago, but it works just as well today as it did back then. In fact, it would seem to be the ruling principle of the kingdom of God. Ask God to help you bring your own life to a new level of peace on earth. You have nothing but heartache to lose and everything, including love and joy, to gain.

Jesus said: "Just as you want men to do to you,
you also do to them likewise."
LUKE 6:31 NKJV

THE WORLD SAYS:

"Sex is just a casual form of recreation."

GOD SAYS:

"Sex is a pure expression of love within the bounds of marriage."

Because there is so much sexual immorality, each man should have his own wife, and each woman should have her own husband.

1 Corinthians 7:2 NLT

On the surface, sex looks smart, sophisticated, and fun. What's wrong with enjoying it—as long as you're careful? You know how to protect yourself from STDs and unwanted pregnancy. You wouldn't do it with just anybody, but only with someone you've gotten to know fairly well. Besides, if you've been dating someone for a while, people assume you're sleeping together anyway. And who knows? This relationship might lead to marriage after all.

Yes, on the surface, sex outside of marriage looks almost innocent. But God sees beneath the surface. He understands your physical desires, your need for closeness, and your yearning to love and be loved. He should—He created you. Unless a special circumstance or God's calling leads you to choose single life, God intends for you to enjoy an active, healthy, and pleasurable sex life. Your sexuality is one of God's many gifts to you. And that's precisely why He tells you how to use it.

In marriage, the God-given and natural sex act joins a man and a woman together physically and spiritually. When there's no binding commitment between the two, however, sex simply appeases their passing physical appetites. The spirit of both goes hungry. Emotional reservations inherent in the choice to "not commit" rob both men and women of the full and satisfying experience God has in mind for them. Perhaps one of your friends has mentioned the fundamental emptiness, the basic disappointment, of uncommitted sex. Perhaps you're familiar with the feeling yourself. If so, reflect on how you view your sexuality. Meditate on what God says about sex, even if what He says goes against your most intense desires. Ask Him for the will and wisdom to follow His plan for your life.

Take God's gift to you—your sexuality—with unreserved gratitude and unbridled delight. Just remember to follow His instructions about how to use it!

Honor marriage, and guard the sacredness of sexual intimacy between wife and husband. God draws a firm line against casual and illicit sex.

Hebrews 13:4 msg

THE WORLD SAYS:
*"Our marriage is over.
I don't love you anymore."*

GOD SAYS:
*"Love is a decision, and
marriage is for a lifetime."*

*Jesus said, "Because God created this organic union of the two sexes,
no one should desecrate his art by cutting them apart."*
MATTHEW 19:6 MSG

"And they lived happily ever after." God knows—He really does—that the stuff of fairy tales and love songs bears little resemblance to what happens in real life. Differences over money, work, and recreation squelch "happy," and poof!—enchantment's over. End of story. Once sweet, "our love" gradually sours to "what love?"

At this point, plenty of couples call it quits. She doesn't feel the way she once did for her husband. He finds someone who interests him more than his wife. If a husband and wife base marriage on a foundation of feelings, they'll soon wake up to find their marriage without a foundation. Feelings—even loving ones—fade. They ebb and flow. They falter, sway, and waver.

Yet feelings—loving feelings—can deepen. Loving feelings can mature and intensify. They can face, endure, and defeat overwhelming odds and the most daunting of life's trials. Loving feelings can do all that—but not loving feelings alone. Loving feelings anchored firmly to a foundation of solemn commitment—marriage—are feelings with "forever" power.

No guarantees exist in marriage nor in any other human condition. God forgives divorce, as He does any other misstep. His intention for married couples, however, is true love that strengthens with time and matures through each season of wedded life. When couples place God at the foundation of marriage, they have Someone to help, comfort, nourish, uphold, and bless them, whatever the day may bring. No one struggles for "his way" or "her way," but both surrender to "God's way." In God-based and God-centered marriages, couples reap the rewards of faithfulness to each other—mature love, mutual friendship, stability, peace, and a lifetime of shared memories.

If you are married, or if you are contemplating marriage, invite God. Give your feelings of love the chance and the challenge to grow into something strong, something sturdy—something forever.

> *Jesus said, "Therefore what God has joined together,*
> *let not man separate."*
>
> Mark 10:9 nkjv

THE WORLD SAYS:
"Just charge it."

GOD SAYS:
"Owe no man anything except the debt of love."

Let love be your only debt! If you love others,
you have done all that the Law demands.

Romans 13:8 cev

You're deep in debt. But your debt has nothing to do with the way you handle money or the score on your credit report. Your debt remains, whether you live on easy street or struggle to meet your basic needs. In addition, your debt requires daily payment, but it's never paid off!

Every Christian carries the same load of debt. Christians recognize God's hand in all they have, including their life and breath. Their debt of gratitude, offered to God in worship, prayer, and praise, acknowledges that life, the world, and all good things come from Him. For all His gifts, God deserves honor and praise! But God doesn't simply sit back and soak up the compliments. He invites His people to put legs—and hands and hearts—on their gratitude by paying the debt of love to everyone.

Of course, the world would rather have you focus your full attention on your wants and desires. In a no-money-now culture, getting things now is painless. Why wait? "I'll pay it off later." The downside of this popular line of thinking generally comes sooner. That expected bonus didn't happen, but a medical emergency did. That job fell through, but the car still needs repairs. Bills add up while stress multiplies. Creditors increase. Payments on the debt of love dwindle to zero.

God has better math for you to live by. He says, "Don't spend above your means. Don't put yourself in a position where you owe money to a crowd of creditors. Instead, focus on Me and all I have done for you. Then pay to others your debt of love."

Start making payments now. Pay yourself well with worthy values, productive work, and self-control. Pay others generously with gentle words, practical help, and genuine friendship. Today, gladly take on your God-given debt of love.

Better one handful with tranquillity than two handfuls
with toil and chasing after the wind.

ECCLESIASTES 4:6

THE WORLD SAYS:
"You have a right to be happy."

GOD SAYS:
"True happiness comes from surrendering your rights to Me."

He who heeds the word wisely will find good,
and whoever trusts in the Lord, happy is he.

PROVERBS 16:20 NKJV

Perhaps things aren't going smoothly right now. You don't have enough money. Your relationships lack excitement. Or maybe you can't pinpoint any specific reason. You're just down in the dumps most days. If only you were somewhere else, with someone else, and in possession of something else, you would be happy.

The world has recommendations. Buy this! Be there! Do it! For a significant portion of your time, effort, and money—especially money—the world offers you whatever will make you happy. The world comes through, too. Upon receiving some wished-for thing, or doing something you really want to do, you naturally feel happy. But as you already know, the happiness doesn't last.

In the Bible, God shows what He does about happiness. First, He gives life. He has blessed you with life, breath, and everything you have. Second, He is compassionate. He seeks you out. He looks for you, not to wag His finger at you, but to love you—because God is love. So you can experience His love, He has put in your heart questions prompting you to look to Him for answers. Third, He gave you the right to be happy. In fact, He sent His Son, Jesus, to show you how to find true and lasting happiness.

Jesus knew suffering here on earth. He could have opted out. His trials, however, did not move Him away from His earthly mission. He didn't seek temporary happiness outside God's plan for His life. Instead, He surrendered Himself to God's will. As an example for Christians down through the ages, Jesus accepted the blessings God granted and the hardships He permitted and gave thanks for both.

Claim your God-given right to happiness by asking God to show you His will for your life. Believe in Him and discover His good plans for your true, lasting, and complete happiness.

Behold, we call those happy who were steadfast. You have heard of the steadfastness of Job, and you have seen the purpose of the Lord, how the Lord is compassionate and merciful.

JAMES 5:11 RSV

THE WORLD SAYS:
"You can't help the way you act."

GOD SAYS:
"Every person will be held responsible for his or her actions."

Be sure to do what you should, for then you will enjoy the personal satisfaction of having done your work well, and you won't need to compare yourself to anyone else. For we are each responsible for our own conduct.

GALATIANS 6:4–5 NLT

Gone are the days when doctors routinely consigned mental patients to a madhouse. Gone, too, are superstitions that relegated unstable minds to the realm of the devil. Developments in the fields of psychiatry and medicine have produced drugs and therapies to counteract many types of mental illnesses. Modern theories explain mental retardation and diseases in scientific terms, citing brain chemistry, genetics, deterioration, or traumatic injury. Surely no one would accuse an Alzheimer's victim of willful wickedness. No credible teacher would expect the same behavior of a Down's syndrome child and a mentally gifted child.

Developments working in favor of some, however, offer others an excuse to disclaim personal responsibility. Rather than learn to curb impulses, take a pill. As an alternative to building strong character, offer weak excuses. Instead of changing negative behavior, accept it as a fixed part of the psyche. "It's just me. I can't help it."

God wants you to turn away from every sort of destructive habit, addiction, or obsession and take responsibility for your actions. He knows the chemistry of your brain, and He's familiar with the nooks and crannies of your mind. He's aware of your childhood, education, and abilities. He has given you free will to make decisions. And He understands your limitations, what hinders you, what scares you, what makes you act the way you do.

God also knows you can't make lasting, effective change on your own. He sends His Holy Spirit to give you the power to take responsibility for your life. If you need help, Christian ministers and mental health professionals can guide you. Doctors and psychiatrists can prescribe any needed medications. Be prepared to drop excuses. With God's help, take responsibility for who you are and what you do.

Even a child is known by his actions,
by whether his conduct is pure and right.

PROVERBS 20:11

THE WORLD SAYS:
"You're ugly and unattractive."

GOD SAYS:
"You are beautiful in My eyes."

The king is enthralled by your beauty;
honor him, for he is your lord.
Psalm 45:11

In the world's eyes, you may or may not be considered beautiful. And perhaps something about your physical appearance bothers you, no matter what other people say.

God has blessed you with certain physical characteristics. It's true, some people seem a bit more blessed than others; but in God's eyes, you are as beautiful as anyone else on this earth. That's because He's looking at the real you. His eyes see the kind of person you are, a matter of far more importance than your height, weight, or hair color.

The Bible offers few descriptions of what particular people actually looked like. Rather, you get to know them by what their actions say about them. The prophet Isaiah preached God's Word, even though few people listened to him. Jesus' disciple Peter declared loyalty to Jesus, then denied even knowing Him when danger threatened. Jesus, for His part, forgave Peter. When sisters Mary and Martha welcomed Jesus into their home, Mary sat down to learn from Him while Martha busied herself in the kitchen. The early-church missionary Paul fearlessly endured persecution for his faith, while Lydia, a businesswoman, turned her house into a meeting place for Christians. Actions speak louder than looks!

Certainly, do what you can to look and feel your best. A well-groomed, attractive appearance bolsters confidence and expresses respect for the people you meet and the places you go. But striving for some sort of physical perfection wastes your time, energy, and money. When you have a godly heart, your actions make you beautiful. The things you do and say leave a lasting mark of beauty wherever you go. In God's eyes—and in everyone else's—you are beautiful.

Stand tall. Put a smile on your face—and get busy being beautiful!

Let the loveliness of our Lord, our God, rest on us, confirming the work that we do. Oh, yes. Affirm the work that we do!
PSALM 90:17 MSG

THE WORLD SAYS:
"It's not a person;
it's just a fetus."

GOD SAYS:
"Before I formed you in your
mother's womb, I knew you."

God said, "Before I shaped you in the womb, I knew all about you.
Before you saw the light of day, I had holy plans for you."

JEREMIAH 1:5 MSG

Violent demonstrations, ugly epithets, and even premeditated murder fill the gulf between pro-life and pro-choice groups. Pro-lifers say personhood begins at conception; therefore, the intentional taking of that life constitutes murder. Pro-choice adherents argue that personhood begins sometime in the later stages of pregnancy, so abortion is merely a medical procedure. The seemingly unbridgeable gap only widens as medical advances allow a pregnant woman to know the sex, health, and mental state of her developing— what? Fetus or child? Pregnant words, both of them.

Jeremiah, a powerful preacher and prophet in seventh-century BC Judea, received a message from God. In it, God told him, "I knew you before you were even conceived. Way before you were born, I had plans for you." For Christians, Jeremiah's testimony and the Psalmist's references to the human qualities of unborn children prove conclusively: Human life begins at conception—and in God's eyes, even before conception!

Now comes the core issue. God highly values human life. He anticipates it, He creates it, and He has plans for each one. Yet, in the name of personal choice, individual freedom, and self-direction, many women seek abortions. Friends stand by and support their decision. Husbands and boyfriends feel relieved, now free of responsibility. Never mind a woman's later pain of loss, her guilt, her recurring nightmares—even her regrets. Medication or therapy can cover all that up, the world assures her.

The Creator of life values life. He values the life of an unborn child as much as He values your life. If you have had an abortion or have helped a woman obtain one, ask God for His forgiveness, comfort, and peace. If you find yourself facing an unwanted pregnancy, take your most desperate issues and darkest fears to Him in prayer. He knows you. He knew you even before you were born. He can—and will— help you now.

The Lord, your Redeemer and Creator, says: "I am the Lord, who made all things. I alone stretched out the heavens. By myself I made the earth and everything in it."

Isaiah 44:24 nlt

THE WORLD SAYS:
"Faith is a private matter."

GOD SAYS:
"You are the light of the world."

Jesus said, "Here's another way to put it: You're here to be light, bringing out the God-colors in the world. God is not a secret to be kept. We're going public with this, as public as a city on a hill."

MATTHEW 5:14 MSG

TRUTH.

Some people will do anything to avoid the limelight. Give a speech? "I'd rather get a root canal!" Head a committee? "Ask someone else." Talk about a relationship with Jesus? "No. My faith is between my God and me."

God, however, says something else. In His ministry on earth, Jesus brought physical light by restoring sight to the blind. He brought spiritual light by preaching God's love for all humanity. Then He told His disciples, "You are the light of the world." Whether they like it or not, Christians stand in light. In fact, they are light!

Christian faith works like a candle. A candle's flame gives out light and warmth, but not without oxygen. Put a lid on a burning candle, and you snuff it out. The flame of faith gives out light and warmth. It feeds on the "oxygen" of communication, interaction, testimony, and experience. Its light spreads through words. Its warmth reaches through actions. A bottled-up private faith has nothing to grow on. It lessens with time. Sometimes it even goes out altogether.

Perhaps the flame of your faith has been burning a long time. Or maybe you are just beginning to feel its first flickers, to know its awakening light, to touch its growing warmth. Either way, give it oxygen! Get it out into the dark world. Fan it by talking about Jesus, testing His promises, studying His Word, sharing His message. Bring others into the welcome warmth of forgiveness, comfort, and love. You never know—your few words, your thoughtful action, your Spirit-led insight, just might be the spark that lights the flame of faith for someone else.

It's okay if you'd choose the root canal over a public speaking engagement—or if you thrive on stage in front of a full house. No matter. You have light. You are light. Whatever you do, start glowing!

The light shines in the darkness,
and the darkness did not comprehend it.

JOHN 1:5 NKJV

THE WORLD SAYS:
"Just move in together. You don't need a piece of paper to prove your love."

GOD SAYS:
"There is no love without commitment."

A man leaves his father and mother and embraces his wife. They become one flesh.

GENESIS 2:24 MSG

Who cares if you just move in together? If you're a young adult, your parents might put up a little fuss, but there's little they can do about it. If your neighbors whisper behind their window shades, so what? If you belong to a church, the pastor will probably look the other way. Your friends see nothing wrong with the arrangement because everyone's doing it. And, no, you don't need a piece of paper to prove your love.

God cares, however, if you just move in together. Neither governing councils nor social custom originated the idea of marriage. Men didn't think it up as a way to subjugate women. Women didn't invent it as a means to capture men. God Himself created marriage. In a perfect world—before the fall into sin—God brought Adam and Eve into a lifelong union. God designed the distinctive relationship of marriage to join a man and a woman together in sexual and emotional intimacy. No other relationship compares to marriage—and no other relationship should attempt to mimic marriage.

Marriage means commitment, though. Many people fear commitment and avoid it. They equate commitment with "tied down," "monotonous," or "inflexible." God doesn't. In His eyes, marriage means a promise to build your life on the foundation He has given couples for their mutual comfort, strength, stability, and companionship. Marriage, far from a simple certificate, publicly declares the respect you have for yourself and for your spouse—and your willingness to put God's will first in your life.

God cares. He cares for you enough to say no to the God-given intimacy of marriage outside the God-given commitment of marriage. He cares for you enough to say no to letting someone take the most intimate aspect of you with no real commitment to you. God cares if you move in together. Shouldn't the two of you?

Be subject to one another out of reverence for Christ.
Ephesians 5:21 rsv

THE WORLD SAYS:

"Let everyone see your good works."

GOD SAYS:

"Give in secret, and I will reward you."

"When you help someone out, don't think about how it looks. Just do it—quietly and unobtrusively. That is the way your God, who conceived you in love, working behind the scenes, helps you out."

MATTHEW 6:3–4 MSG

Christianity puts a great deal of emphasis on human behavior—with good reason. Its history reaches back to Moses on Mount Sinai receiving from God His Ten Commandments. In His ministry on earth, Jesus spoke often and specifically about actions expected of His followers and those forbidden to His followers. Unfortunately, many Christians remember only the "what" of good works and forget the all-important "why."

Christians and non-Christians alike value—and per-form—good works. Kind words, neighborly help, and generous gifts to charity aren't the sole province of believers in Jesus. Good-hearted people of different faiths and of no faith do those things and more. Christians differentiate them-selves not by their good works, but why they do them. And the "why"—motivation—is the secret known only to God and the individual Christian.

Good deeds done for show, to garner admiration, to earn goodwill, high grades, or fat bonuses fail God's scrutiny. Those who act for these reasons get rewarded by the people they manage to impress. Piety for the purpose of earning God's approval sadly—and tragically—achieves nothing. An attempt to earn God's favor is futile from the onset. Jesus, God's Son, earned God's approval for everyone through the mystery of His suffering, death, and resurrection. Believers, through faith in Him, stand guilt-free in front of God now and for eternity. You have God's approval because of Jesus.

Yes, God has given you Himself. His love at work in your life gives you the motivation to do productive, helpful, kind, and God-pleasing things. Whether your good works are ap-plauded by crowds or appreciated only by an infant, seen by many or remembered by no one, met with thanks or indiffer-ence, do them simply because you know the "secret" of God's great love for you. And He promises to reward you openly.

The Lord said, "I the Lord search the heart and examine the mind, to reward a man according to his conduct, according to what his deeds deserve."

JEREMIAH 17:10

THE WORLD SAYS:
"Go ahead and sin;
God will forgive you."

GOD SAYS:
"Repent and sin no more."

*[Jesus] said to her, "Woman, where are these accusers of yours? Has
no one condemned you?" She said, "No one, Lord." And Jesus said
to her, "Neither do I condemn you; go and sin no more."*

JOHN 8:10–11 NKJV

In the beginning years of the Christian church, the missionary Paul tackled the world's argument: Go ahead and sin; God will forgive you. After all, if someone accepts God's full and complete forgiveness through faith in Jesus Christ, isn't that person then free to act in any way he or she desires? Most assuredly, yes. But will a repentant and forgiven child of God desire sinful things? Absolutely not!

When God's grace frees a believer from the power of sin, sin no longer rules the believer. The believer no longer serves under cruel masters, such as addictions, destructive thoughts and actions, pornography, and deviant sexual desires. Christ took sin—all sin—to the grave with Him. In the mystery of His death on the cross, those masters now stand powerless in the lives of repentant, forgiven sinners. Believers live in the light of Christ's resurrection from the grave, in the light of His righteousness, in the light of His grace. Light! Why would anyone want to step back into darkness?

Yet, sin stalks even the most fervent believers. Temptation lures with the suggestion of a quick peek…one more drink… just to try it…only this time. Habitual behaviors prove difficult to change. Today's circumstances clamor for yesterday's response, just because it feels comfortable to do what you've always done—comfort at the cost of freedom.

God forgives sin, even the one you do over and over again. The sin you're not sure you're able to leave behind. The sin no one even suspects of you. Yes, even that one. Repent of all sin. Turn to the One who frees you. The new life Christ offers you comes with His power to turn away from sin. His Spirit strengthens you to take and live the freedom He has won for you. In Christ, go…and sin no more.

It is for freedom that Christ has set us free. Stand firm, then, and do not let yourselves be burdened again by a yoke of slavery.

GALATIANS 5:1

THE WORLD SAYS:
"Align yourself with the rich and powerful."

GOD SAYS:
"The meek will inherit the earth."

Jesus said, "You're blessed when you're content with just who you are—no more, no less. That's the moment you find yourselves proud owners of everything that can't be bought."

MATTHEW 5:5 MSG

In today's economy, meekness doesn't cut it. Go-getters go after the best schools, the best jobs, the top posts of their profession. High achievers align themselves with people able to help them reach their goals. They connect themselves with the rich and powerful because those are the people pulling the strings that make things happen. Is it wrong to put yourself forward as a bright, hardworking, achievement-oriented person? No. But at the same time, put on an attitude of meekness—Christian meekness. It's anything but timid!

Christian meekness expresses itself in robust and courageous action. It doesn't pander to the powerful and scorn the weak; it treats everyone with dignity and respect. It never peers over the head of a low-ranking clerk to catch the eye of the CEO; it greets both with warmth and sincerity. It often occupies positions of status and power, yet by no means does it stomp around in a fit of anger if an underling fails to show proper deference. Christian meekness acknowledges the efforts and seeks the opinions of those lower in rank or importance, wealth or influence. Christian meekness heartily accepts well-earned promotions, rewards, accolades, and honors with confident grace and humble gratitude.

God declares the meek will inherit the earth. Jesus gives Christians permission to use rightly earned material possessions—including status, power, and influence—with saintly self-assurance. Instead of jealously guarding rank and wealth against all comers, the meek Christian confidently and fully employs everything he or she receives with thanks to God, the Giver of all good things. Spirit-filled meekness never shivers in the shadows; it celebrates the happiness of receiving, having, and using God's material gifts.

Are you ambitious? Don't hold back—go for it! Reach for the stars with the robust, courageous strength of the meek!

The meek shall inherit the land, and delight themselves in
abundant prosperity.
Psalm 37:11 nrsv

THE WORLD SAYS:
*"We are all brothers
and sisters."*

GOD SAYS:
*"Those who obey Me are My
brothers and sisters."*

*Jesus said, "Anyone who obeys my Father in heaven
is my brother or sister or mother."*
MATTHEW 12:50 CEV

Jesus, the Son of God, was born into a human family. One time during His public ministry, His mother and brothers approached the house where He was preaching. Someone elbowed his way to the front of the crowd surrounding Jesus and informed Him, "Your mother and brothers want to talk to You." Jesus used the occasion to tell His listeners: "You are My mother, brothers, and sisters. Everyone obedient to Me is obedient to My Father in heaven. And if you do the will of my Father in heaven, then you are My mother, brother, and sister" (see Matthew 12:46–50).

In no way did Jesus intend to devalue the special bond between parents and children, between brothers and sisters, among relatives. Rather, He pointed out that these earthly family relationships mean little as far as a believer's relationship to Him. Who your parents are or what they did doesn't matter in God's family. Your family name won't earn you privileges. What counts is your personal obedience to God's will, and God's will is that you believe in His Son, Jesus Christ.

Jesus' present-day mother, brothers, and sisters boldly and confidently go to Him, as freely as anyone approaches a beloved family member. Many times in the Bible, Jesus opens His arms to His disciples, calling them into close relationship with Him. God is no distant deity sitting in the sky and watching the world spin through space. Instead, He actively invites you into relationship with Him—a family relationship. Jesus urges you to call Him "Brother" and to call His Father in heaven your Father.

Your relationship with Jesus brings you into spiritual unity with other believers. Your mother, brothers, and sisters in Christ serve you with encouragement, help, fellowship, and spiritual nourishment. What do you need? Ask. In Christ, it's a family thing—and you're family!

Those whom he foreknew he also predestined to be conformed
to the image of his Son, in order that he might be
the firstborn within a large family.

ROMANS 8:29 NRSV

THE WORLD SAYS:

"You have to work all the time to get ahead."

GOD SAYS:

"I have created one day each week for rest."

God blessed the seventh day. He made it a Holy Day because on that day he rested from his work, all the creating God had done.

GENESIS 2:3 MSG

Whatever 24/7 does for convenience, it shatters tranquility. When you know the gym's open all night, why not work out at 2 a.m.? Since shops stay open all day Sunday, why not get a part-time retail job and earn some extra money? If you're not working, networking, or at least keeping up with the latest movies, you'll never get ahead! The frantic faces of people scurrying from one place to the next, armed with their daily planner, cell phone, and overloaded satchel attest to a pervasive anxiety about time.

Every day, health care professionals diagnose the consequences of overextended schedules, on-the-go meals, and too little rest. Indigestion, insomnia, headaches, irritability, along with fatigue-related accidents, often result from overwork. Instead of getting ahead, the go-getter gets laid up in bed.

God created time and allotted it equally to each person, rich or poor, nine months old or ninety. And as with any other of His gifts, God included user instructions. Even more, He modeled His instructions Himself. The biblical account of creation reveals that God created the world in six days and rested on the seventh. Certainly overwhelming fatigue wasn't the reason for His rest. As awesome as His work of creation was, He blessed His day of rest and declared it holy. He set an example. No matter how important your work is, no matter how pressing your responsibilities are, rest is mandatory. Your body needs it. Even more important, your soul requires it.

Today, opt out of 24/7 frenzy. Balance your work and responsibilities with fixed times for worship, fellowship, and personal spiritual refreshment. Perhaps you will need to rethink your priorities and make difficult choices. But rest—a holy time—is more than a choice you make for yourself. It's the choice God, in His goodness, made for you.

The Lord said, "I will refresh the weary and satisfy the faint."
JEREMIAH 31:25

THE WORLD SAYS:
"Being a Christian is too hard."

GOD SAYS:
"My yoke is easy, and My burden is light."

Jesus said, "Are you tired? Worn out? Burned out on religion? Come to me. Get away with me and you'll recover your life. I'll show you how to take a real rest. Walk with me and work with me—watch how I do it. Learn the unforced rhythms of grace. I won't lay anything heavy or ill-fitting on you. Keep company with me and you'll learn to live freely and lightly."

MATTHEW 11:28–30 MSG

If being a Christian seems hard, think how hard it is not being a Christian. Burdened by guilt, non-Christians have several options available: (1) Initiate changes in thought and behavior in hopes of attaining personal flawlessness, (2) Smother guilt with denial or distractions, (3) Rename sin ("mistake" is a likely candidate) so it doesn't result in those prickly feelings of guilt. If you hunger after a high-maintenance spiritual regimen, pick one of these choices. Or not.

Sin infects the world and affects everyone in the world. Natural disasters, wars, terrorism, murders, and crime all stem from it. Human thoughts, words, actions, intentions, and motivations are rooted in it. No self-prescribed program of perfection can rid anyone of it or the guilt of it. God sees through whitewash. No amount of denial or make-believe has the power to diminish or dismiss its seriousness. Whatever people choose to call it, God calls it sin.

Jesus challenges every person to recognize his or her sinfulness. Those who honestly confront their sin and the weight of guilt they bear because of it know they're carrying a burden too heavy to handle alone. Those humble enough to confess their sin, to plead for forgiveness, know that no human contrivance can answer them. To these—to you—Jesus says, "Come."

Come. Jesus never promised the absence of sin-produced struggles in this life. He did promise, however, to ease the yoke of sin by removing guilt and eternal punishment. He promised to lighten the burden of guilt by giving believers the ability to turn from sin and receive His forgiveness.

God promises you an easy yoke and a light burden. Why not get down on your knees and trade your burdens for His today? You'll stand up a lot lighter!

I wait quietly before God, for my salvation comes from him.
He alone is my rock and my salvation, my fortress where
I will never be shaken.

PSALM 62:1–2 NLT

THE WORLD SAYS:
"Walk past the poor.
They're just lazy."

GOD SAYS:
"He who reaches out to the
lowest members of society
reaches out to Me."

Jesus said, "Anyone who gives you a cup of water in my name, just
because you belong to me, will surely be rewarded."

MARK 9:41 CEV

In the aftermath of a catastrophic event, people respond with notable compassion. Outpourings of prayers, sympathy, food, and medicines flow to victims. Unrelenting newscasters cover the situation, interviewing survivors standing in front of a backdrop of disaster. When the spotlight's on, people reach out with generosity.

Outside the range of lights and cameras, however, helping hands withdraw. The scruffy panhandler downtown. The disheveled woman who spends her days on a park bench. The husky-looking young man who's unemployed. The single mom living on welfare. The family dogged by debt. From these individuals, eyes turn away. Checkbooks shut. Harsh judgment replaces simple kindness.

During Jesus' ministry on earth, many who witnessed His miracles decided He was the answer to their social problems. After all, He conferred instant health on the sick. He multiplied loaves and fish to feed a crowd and could even produce water-turned-wine to wash it down. But these same people failed to get His point. His miracles spotlighted not His candidacy for food king, but His authority as God. His miracles dramatically displayed God's compassion for individuals, especially the poor in health and in spirit. Jesus was not unaware of the unwise choices individuals can make. Jesus knew the personal and the social forces that drive some people down to the lowest levels of society and keep them there. Nonetheless, He reached out with help. Practical help. Individual help, when and where needed.

Jesus set an example of effective compassion and active kindness. Guided by His Spirit, try dispensing some of it yourself. You can work miracles with a visit to an elderly person—your grandma, perhaps—who's "poor" for lack of a friendly face. You can spare a few minutes to speak to the office cleaning woman who's "poor" for lack of respect. In Christ, reach out to just one…and reach out to Him.

He who is kind to the poor lends to the Lord, and he will reward
him for what he has done.

Proverbs 19:17

THE WORLD SAYS:
"God doesn't want me anyway."

GOD SAYS:
"I'm not willing for anyone to perish, but all to come to the truth."

God loved the people of this world so much that he gave his only Son, so that everyone who has faith in him will have eternal life and never really die.

JOHN 3:16 CEV

So what in the world would God want with you? Perhaps a cynical friend has noted your interest in Christianity by sneering at the incomprehensibility of the God of the universe sending you—you, of all people!—a divine invitation. And deep down inside, you might be wondering the same thing.

No one can claim himself or herself a worthy subject of God's attention. Yet, throughout the Bible, God declares His love for individuals, for nations, indeed for the whole world. God shows His love in the person and ministry of Jesus, the promised Messiah. Jesus demonstrated God's love to individuals, preached God's truth to crowds, and sent God's invitation throughout the world with the gift of His Holy Spirit. To complete God's plan for the salvation of all people, Jesus died on the cross and rose from the grave on behalf of all people.

Individuals, however, possess free will. God's plan for the salvation of the world can be disbelieved, His love refused, His very existence doubted. People who choose not to accept God often lay the blame on God, claiming "God doesn't want me anyway." With that, the nonbeliever exempts himself or herself from listening to God's clear declarations and unmistakable actions to the contrary. God permits godlessness, and sin promotes it.

God has already made it clear He wants you to come to the knowledge of the truth. His Spirit at work in you has given you the desire to discover more about Him. And the more you find out about Him, the more you discover His love for you…His personal care for you…His plan for you to know His truth.

So why in the world does the God of the universe want you? Because He loves the world and everyone in it. He invites you to get as near to Him as He is to you. Your response is most sincerely requested.

The Lord is not slow in keeping his promise, as some understand slowness. He is patient with you, not wanting anyone to perish, but everyone to come to repentance.

2 PETER 3:9

THE WORLD SAYS:
"There's plenty more where that came from."

GOD SAYS:
"Be wise stewards of all the earth's resources."

God gave them his blessing and said: Have a lot of children! Fill the earth with people and bring it under your control. Rule over the fish in the ocean, the birds in the sky, and every animal on the earth.

GENESIS 1:28 CEV

Environmental protection is not so much a matter of secular ecology but of Christian theology. God created the world and everything in it. He put human beings in charge of His creation. He declared people caretakers of everything from the riches of the earth to the mysteries of outer space. God has given people authority over animals, plants, trees, minerals, air, and water. If you want to see a caretaker of creation, just look in the mirror!

The magnificent privilege of using and enjoying God's creation carries certain serious responsibilities. God has retained ownership of the world for Himself. He appointed people its caretakers only. How then should earth's caretakers go about their work? Consider the world's dwindling supply of natural resources. Lakes, rivers, and seas polluted by factory waste. Air poisoned by radiation leakages and gas fumes. Overflowing landfills. Thousands of acres of woodlands and wetlands destroyed. Inhumane treatment of animals. On this evidence alone, earth's caretakers could be taken to court and charged with creation abuse.

Environmental protection begins with caretakers willing to take their responsibilities seriously. Voting decisions, letters to the newspaper, and support for environmental causes impact policies and regulations that can affect the environment in positive ways. But the first step rests with the individual caretaker—you. Hold up a mirror to your lifestyle. Is it creation friendly? Do you rightfully use—or wrongfully abuse—the corner of creation in which God has placed you? Is what you're doing now sensitive to the well-being of your neighbor? Of today's children? Of tomorrow's children? Does your lifestyle reflect a caretaker—or simply a taker?

Secular ecology urges you to conserve for a very secular reason: The world doesn't have infinite supplies of natural resources. Christian theology urges good stewardship over all creation for a very Christian reason: It all belongs to God.

It is required that those who have been given a trust must prove faithful.

1 CORINTHIANS 4:2

THE WORLD SAYS:

"You don't need anyone but yourself."

GOD SAYS:

"I've created you to live in unity and community."

If we are living in the light of God's presence, just as Christ is, then we have fellowship with each other, and the blood of Jesus, his Son, cleanses us from every sin.

1 JOHN 1:7 NLT

Christian life has been compared to a cross. The vertical beam represents a Christian's central, grounded, "straight-up" relationship to God. The horizontal beam depicts a Christian's extended, embracing, "straight-across" relationship to other Christians. It's an apt symbol. God never intended the Christian life to be lived in isolation from other believers.

Certainly faith in Christ comes to each believer individually. Grounded in the truths of scripture, faith grows upward to ever-increasing heights of praise, gratitude, trust, and devotion. But taken only this far, faith lacks real-life application. If it's largely a private matter, faith receives no encouragement, nourishment, and support from other Christians. This faith may indeed praise God, but not completely and fully the way God intends.

God gives the light of faith to one person so that person can be a light for and among others. Lively, light-producing faith cannot help but extend outward in active Christian fellowship. Stemming from a personal relationship to Jesus Christ through faith, Christians desire to exercise and share faith, deepen and expand faith, among and with people of faith. Their communal "straight-across" fellowship with one another in turn increases the strength and vitality of their individual "straight-up" relationship with God.

Private devotions and Bible study are essential in a healthy and balanced faith-life. God hears prayers uttered in the secret depths of one heart just as He hears prayers spoken in unison by hundreds or thousands of voices. But don't be satisfied with a faith untested by experience and bereft of the influence of other Christians. Don't let other Christians miss the support and inspiration you have to offer them. Faith gets stronger when it's shared. In faith, as in life, don't try to go it alone. Instead, be a cross. Reach up to God—and reach out to others.

Each of you should look not only to your own interests,
but also to the interests of others.

PHILIPPIANS 2:4

THE WORLD SAYS:
*"God knows
I'm not perfect."*

GOD SAYS:
*"You are holy because
I am holy."*

Be perfect, therefore, as your heavenly Father is perfect.
Matthew 5:48

A mother's extraordinary demands for achievement discourage her children. A manager's intimidating prerequisites for promotion dishearten his employees. A professor's lofty requirements for an A cause her students to give up hope. Jesus' clear insistence on faultlessness must have made many of His hearers walk away in dismay. Does the Teacher have a clue? Nobody's perfect!

Yet many people have taken on themselves the mandate to become perfect. Whether a desire to please God, elevate themselves, or impress other people, they adopt an ideal and do everything humanly possible to attain it. Expensive cosmetics and plastic surgeries try to bridge the gap between models' looks and real faces. Ascetic regimens, esoteric rules, and spartan disciplines attempt to close the chasm between heaven and humanity. Result? Either a pitiful illusion of otherworldliness or a sad admission of failure. Nobody's perfect.

Taken as an isolated statement, Jesus' command would panic even His most ardent followers, perhaps even leading them toward some impossible dream. Taken as part of His plan for believers, however, His command becomes an exciting invitation, an opportunity offered in love. Jesus, fully human and fully God, did what no human being could ever possibly do: He lived a perfect life here on earth. He offered Himself as a stand-in for all humanity when He died for the sins of the world. He rose from the grave to prove the effectiveness of His sacrifice. He won for all the privilege of perfection—His perfection. Christ bridged the great divide between holiness and you.

Be holy! Be perfect! It's not too much to ask, because through faith in Christ, you have His perfection. However imperfectly you will do it, He looks with pleasure on the many ways you put His perfection into practice.

Just as [God] who called you is holy, so be holy in all you do;
for it is written: "Be holy, because I am holy."

1 PETER 1:15–16

THE WORLD SAYS:
"Church is a big bore."

GOD SAYS:
"Don't forget how important it is to meet with other believers."

Some people have gotten out of the habit of meeting for worship, but we must not do that. We should keep on encouraging each other, especially since you know that the day of the Lord's coming is getting closer.

HEBREWS 10:25 CEV

If you find yourself getting nothing out of church, it's time to ask: *What am I putting into church?* It might surprise you to learn that church doesn't simply ask for your attendance. Church requires your participation.

First, participate by leaving. Leaving? Yes. As soon as you sit down, leave your burdens at the foot of Jesus' cross. Name your worries, guilt, cares, and stresses. In your mind, wrap them in a bundle and give the whole thing to your Lord and Savior. He has promised to pick it up—no matter how heavy it is—and leave you with the lightness of His peace.

Second, participate by listening. With your mind fully engaged, listen to the reading of scripture. Listen to the message spoken by the minister. Listen to yourself as you sing hymns and recite prayers. Then prepare to be amazed! The Holy Spirit works through the readings, message, hymns, and prayers to remove doubts, answer questions, soothe unrest, and ease anxiety. Actively open yourself to the work He wants to accomplish in you.

Third, participate by meeting others. Get to know the people with whom you worship. You might be the one God has sent to offer a much-needed compliment to a person still reeling from a particularly difficult week. Someone else might be the one through whom God will give you the blessing of friendship. You'll never know unless you're willing to smile, shake hands, and share a few good words with the people around you.

Go to a church where the Word of God is preached. Meditate on the awesome mystery of His gift to you, Jesus Christ. Think deeply. He willingly and actively gave His life for you. Actively participate in your response of thanksgiving, praise, and worship in the company of His beloved people. You won't get bored. Tired maybe—but never bored.

Let the words of Christ, in all their richness, live in your hearts and make you wise. Use his words to teach and counsel each other. Sing psalms and hymns and spiritual songs to God with thankful hearts.

COLOSSIANS 3:16 NLT

THE WORLD SAYS:
"Some things are too hard to bear."

GOD SAYS:
"My grace is sufficient for you."

Jesus said to me, "My grace is sufficient for you, for My strength is made perfect in weakness." Therefore most gladly I will rather boast in my infirmities, that the power of Christ may rest upon me.

2 Corinthians 12:9 nkjv

The most difficult part of life often consists not in troubles from outside, but from turmoil going on inside. "How can I claim to be a Christian when everyone knows my weaknesses…my personality flaws…how many mistakes I've made? God certainly can't use me—just look at my record of messing things up!"

The apostle Paul, a tireless missionary and diligent pastor in the early Church, suffered a personal weakness he called "a thorn in the flesh." The Bible doesn't say exactly what it was, though many theologians suggest malaria. Three times Paul prayed to God for deliverance. Presumably, Paul's ministry would have been all the more vigorous if he had been free of this thing that slowed him down and made him appear feeble in the eyes of others. But God said, "No, Paul. You have everything you need. You have My grace." By God's grace, Paul continued God's work despite his limiting and humbling thorn in the flesh. In fact, God turned Paul's negative into a positive. If such an obviously weak man could do such tremendous things, surely it's because of the Spirit of God and the strength of God at work in him!

God uses human weaknesses, fears, and failures to show His strength. He uses the things that turn believers to anguished prayer to build up their reliance on Him and His power. Despite the human qualities of His people, He accomplishes His heavenly work through His people. Can any individual believer take credit for work performed, trials borne, or missions accomplished for His sake? No, certainly not. Just look at those thorns!

Face what makes you cringe about yourself. Name the thorn in your flesh. Take it to your Lord in prayer. Sure, ask Him for deliverance. Ask Him again. And again. But if He says no, remember His grace. He can do great things with you, thorns and all.

God is able to make all grace abound to you,
so that in all things at all times, having all that you need,
you will abound in every good work.

2 CORINTHIANS 9:8

THE WORLD SAYS:
"Jesus' return is a fairy tale."

GOD SAYS:
"I will come and receive you to Myself, that where I am you will be also."

Jesus said, "When everything is ready, I will come and get you, so that you will always be with me where I am."

JOHN 14:3 NLT

Many popular books and movies have moved the subject of Jesus' Second Coming out of pulpits and into school hallways, office lounges, and Internet chat rooms. As with any hot topic, information and misinformation mix freely. Pure conjecture weaves in and out of scriptural truth.

Nonbelievers dismiss the whole idea of Jesus' return, the end times, and Judgment Day. Believers accept the Second Coming but bicker over the details. Will He initiate a thousand-year reign? Will He take believers into heaven and leave everyone else scrambling for the meaning of it all? Or will He appear one day and judge everyone, saints and sinners, at the same moment?

A great deal of today's end-time speculation comes from the two letters of the apostle Paul to the Thessalonians and the vision of the apostle John, recorded in the book of Revelation. Many passages in these sections of scripture are mysterious, no doubt about it. Taken out of context, particular passages seem to confirm claims of imaginative storytellers. But neither the entertainment value of fantastic fictions nor the difficulty of interpreting end-time prophecies should deflect your attention from one all-important, rock-solid fact: Jesus will come again.

When Jesus spoke to His disciples of His Second Coming, His words obviously sounded very strange. His disciples asked questions. When? Where? How? His listeners probed for information. But Jesus wasn't telling them of His Second Coming to fill them in on all the details. He talked about it so they could take comfort, courage, and hope from His promise.

It's a fact: Jesus will return. Speculation about specifics wastes time much more wisely spent in preparation for His return. If He came today, would you clap your hands or quake in your boots? What about your friends and loved ones? Are they ready?

Jesus said, "I am coming soon. Hold on to what you have,
so that no one will take your crown."

REVELATION 3:11

THE WORLD SAYS:
"Of course I'm going to heaven. I'm a good person."

GOD SAYS:
"Being good isn't good enough. Only the blood of My Son, Jesus, can qualify you for heaven."

It was not with perishable things such as silver or gold that you were redeemed from the empty way of life handed down to you from your forefathers, but with the precious blood of Christ, a lamb without blemish or defect.

1 PETER 1:18–19

Consumers expect choices. The more, the better. Personalized goods and services cater to consumers' ever-increasing demand for products tailored to their needs and wants. Jesus, however, offered no choice of salvation plans for finicky shoppers. He clearly pointed to Himself as the one way—the only way—to His Father in heaven.

Non-Christians bristle at the suggestion that there's one way to heaven. In the name of tolerance, many Christians deny Jesus' words by throwing open the gates of heaven to all good people, no matter what their beliefs. While well-meaning, these Christians are naively trying to open a gate not theirs to open. God in Jesus Christ opens and closes the gates of heaven.

God's love desires everyone to enter heaven. In His mercy, He didn't make salvation dependent upon an individual's intelligence, goodness, ability, virtue, or circumstances in life. Instead, God sent Jesus from heaven to open the gates of heaven to those who accept the faith His Spirit freely works in them. In this faith, the believer comes to know Jesus as his or her personal Savior.

Every day, people die without having had an opportunity to hear about Jesus and His atoning death and victorious resurrection. God, the Creator of life, will solve all the mysteries of eternal life. Human inability to answer every question about salvation in no way diminishes the truth of Jesus' words. You have heard Him say, "I am the way. You must come through Me." He has chosen you. The only choice you have is to accept Him or reject Him.

Nothing makes Christians superior to other people. By grace He has called them. By the same grace, He calls you. Respond gracefully to Him. Then remember those who have not yet heard and those who do not yet believe.

There is one God; there is also one mediator between God and humankind, Christ Jesus, himself human, who gave himself as ransom for all.

1 TIMOTHY 2:5–6 NRSV

THE WORLD SAYS:

"No one cares how hard you work on behalf of others."

GOD SAYS:

"I see, and I will reward you."

Jesus said, "Love your enemies! Do good to them! Lend to them! And don't be concerned that they might not repay. Then your reward from heaven will be very great, and you will truly be acting as children of the Most High, for he is kind to the unthankful and to those who are wicked."

LUKE 6:35 NLT

If you want to try out for a varsity team or a spot in an orchestra, prepare yourself by practicing. For hours and hours. Every day. It's a seemingly thankless task. You won't receive a rousing cheer at the end of every session. You won't hear a round of applause after an hour's drill on a difficult measure. And whether or not you make the team or secure a chair in the orchestra, you gain the rewards of perseverance, ability to delay gratification, and enhanced skills. The thankless task of practice pays off, regardless of outcome.

The same principle can be applied to the things you do for others. Maybe you know you'll hear the "thank you" later, as when you care for the daily needs of an infant. Or maybe you will never hear a word of gratitude from an elderly and confused relative or patient. Maybe no one seems to notice how clean you keep the house, or the fact that you always wipe up the office lunchroom. Maybe no one saw you get out of your car and remove road debris that could have caused another driver a flat tire. But God, who is everywhere, sees.

Because they know God loved them first and chose them to be His own, believers practice "thank you" in practical ways. Sometimes the ways are open for all to see, and sometimes not. Regardless, God has rewards—the first of which is the dignity of having done the right thing.

What are the thankless tasks in your life? A good word to a crabby neighbor? A patient smile for an overbearing in-law? A respectful attitude toward an egotistical boss or arrogant educator? Go at it gladly and willingly. Then stand ready to receive your rewards from God, the Giver of all good things.

Dear friends, you must never become tired of doing right.
2 Thessalonians 3:13 cev

THE WORLD SAYS:
"Christianity is just a bunch of rules."

GOD SAYS:
"My rules are not to burden you—but to protect you."

Oh, the joys of those who do not follow the advice of the wicked,
or stand around with sinners, or join in with scoffers.
But they delight in doing everything the LORD wants;
day and night they think about his law.

PSALM 1:1–2 NLT

Unless there's an obvious social consequence to breaking them—such as jail—some Christians regard God's rules as optional. But God revealed His Law neither as a source of good advice nor as shackles designed to take all the good times out of life.

God's Law has been compared to a mirror and a curb. As a mirror, God's Law reflects the true human condition and prompts sincere repentance. No one, except Jesus Christ, has ever led a perfectly obedient life. Jesus came to fulfill God's Law by being perfect because no one other than God can be perfect and fulfill the demands of His Law. He knew you couldn't so He took your sins on Himself. In the mystery of His sacrifice on the cross, He completely fulfilled the Law for you. Your repentance brings you the benefits of His death and resurrection: forgiveness and new life in Him.

As a curb, God's Law protects His people. Think about some of the ways the laws of your community protect you, and you get an idea of God's intention. You already follow many of God's and society's rules because you know the results of not doing so. Others of His rules—especially those not part of the legal code—may appear voluntary. They aren't. The absence of obvious bad consequences to any of God's "no's" gives no one the right to challenge God's wisdom. Even if society says it's okay, it isn't okay if God says it's not. Let others learn why God forbids it—eventually and to their sorrow, they will. For you, it's enough to know He does.

Christianity has rules, yes. God put them there because He cares about the kind and quality of life you lead. With His mirror in your hand and His curb at your feet, walk in safety and in certainty...and have the time of your life!

I am your servant, LORD, and you have kept your promise
to treat me with kindness. Give me wisdom and good sense.
I trust your commands.
PSALM 119:65–66 CEV

THE WORLD SAYS:
"I've earned all that I have."

GOD SAYS:
"I have given you the ability to produce wealth."

Remember the LORD your God, for it is he who gives you the ability to produce wealth, and so confirms his covenant, which he swore to your forefathers, as it is today.

DEUTERONOMY 8:18

Houses don't drop from the sky. They're built from the ground up. Work, not wishful thinking, earns money. God gave people talents, skills, and resources that He expects them to use productively and well.

Through hard work, know-how, and opportunity, many people achieve a high level of financial success and social recognition. Perhaps you're one of them, or you're well on the way to building a secure and comfortable life for yourself and your loved ones. Congratulations! But a word of warning: Remember who gave you your building materials.

Thanksgiving to God for your blessings acknowledges Him as Giver of all good things. And gratitude to Him results in real-life, practical benefits to you. First, unhealthy pride and fatuous boasting cannot stand on a foundation of God-centered humility. You'll get to enjoy the sincere respect of those with whom you live and work, which is much more comfortable than provoking anger, bitterness, revenge, and hatred. Second, debilitating fears of failure cannot threaten to fell the walls of your work. You'll get to take pleasure in what you build because you realize God enabled you to build it. It doesn't—and never did—all depend on you. What a relief!

Third, selfishness and insensitivity cannot weaken the integrity of the structure. You'll get to bless others as generously as God has blessed you—that's a thank-you attitude put into action. And fourth, loss cannot devastate the servant who knows God owns the house. You'll get to gratefully accept God's will in all things that may come your way, including personal loss. What peace of mind—better than any insurance contract you'll ever sign.

Look around the "house" He has given you—your talents, your abilities, your resources. Right now, give thanks to the Giver. Then keep on building!

Every house has a builder, but the Builder behind them all is God.
HEBREWS 3:4 MSG

THE WORLD SAYS:
"God is watching us—from a distance."

GOD SAYS:
"I want to have a personal relationship with you, and I'm as close as your breath."

The Lord is close to all who call on him, yes, to all who call on him sincerely.

PSALM 145:18 NLT

Rainstorms flood houses of worship and dens of thieves. Tornadoes flatten the homes of devout Christians and those of professed atheists. People of all religions and of no religion have heard the dreaded diagnosis, "It's cancer." So where is God? Cynics seize the opportunity to question the level of divine control over life. Unbelievers smirk in their certainty that God—if there is a God—couldn't care less about the human condition. Christians come off looking foolishly ignorant. But look again.

God never promised the absence of suffering this side of heaven. He did, however, promise His presence. Not just a passive Guy-in-the-sky presence, but an active I'm-here-for-you, up-close-and-personal presence. Believers suffer and mourn, sure, but faithfully. With their mourning comes a deep awareness of God's closeness. His Spirit restores, rebuilds, and renews. Believers call to God in their time of trial, and from Him they receive hope and strength. Evidence? Ask a Christian who has suffered. In other words, ask any Christian.

God demonstrated His love for the world and His involvement in it when He promised the world a Messiah—that is, One who could satisfy His judgment of sin. Jesus fulfilled God's promise. His life reveals God's compassion and care for individuals. His death and resurrection prove His desire to bring you close. His Spirit at work in you right now shows without a doubt He lives in you. He has enabled you to have a personal relationship with Him.

In good times, call on the One who is as near to you as your breath. And when times are not so good, you'll never have to ask where He is. You'll know He hears your cry for help, not from a distance, but right where you are—wherever you are.

Blessed are those who have learned to acclaim you,
who walk in the light of your presence, O LORD.
PSALM 89:15

TRUTH.

THE WORLD SAYS:
"The Bible isn't relevant for your life today."

GOD SAYS:
"The sum of My Word is truth; My righteous ordinances last forever."

All your words are true; all your righteous laws are eternal.
PSALM 119:160

You've heard spin. Spin doctors twirl facts so you will approve their message. Corporate and governmental blunders require the services of spin doctors to reshape offenses into something at least benign, if not downright positive. Unfortunately, Christians often try to spin the Bible into something other than what it is: the Word of God.

Jesus' disciples attempted spin. They complained to Him about His teachings, many of which they found hard to believe. Peter, one of His closest disciples, urged Jesus to lighten up on the suffering-and-death talk. Because the Lord refused to massage His message to coddle His hearers, some took offense and left Him. Nonetheless, the Word of God and the work of God remained unchanged.

Today, some Christian ministers attempt to make God's message more palatable to contemporary audiences. They omit certain teachings and manipulate others. The seriousness of sin, for example, gets bypassed in favor of a gentle wink at human fallibility. Some theologians take it upon themselves to approve the Bible's reasonable sayings while dismissing the ones deemed unreasonable. Some individual Christians simply decide for themselves what feels comfortable and what doesn't.

God gave His people His revealed Word—the Bible—as a gift. In it, He didn't cater to human curiosity or make every detail fit within the limits of human intelligence. Instead, He inspired writers to record His work and His will for the lives of His people. It's the same saving work and gracefull will for all people of all time. Most specifically, the Bible provides you with a clear testimony of God's attitude toward you: He loves you.

Read your Bible with His Spirit of wisdom and understanding. Meditate on those things you find disturbing or difficult. For help, consult Christian ministers, church leaders, and Christian friends who respect the Bible for what it is—God's eternal, unchanging, and ever-relevant Word.

We have the word of the prophets made more certain, and you will do well to pay attention to it, as to a light shining in a dark place, until the day dawns and the morning star rises in your hearts.

2 PETER 1:19

THE WORLD SAYS:
"Gossip is harmless.
You need to know what's
going on."

GOD SAYS:
"Gossip stirs up dissension
and separates friends."

Troublemakers start fights; gossips break up friendships.
PROVERBS 16:28 MSG

Pssst—just curious. A friend responds with hearsay. A neighbor offers details. A coworker swears it's true.

Gossip builds as sparks of rumor, innuendo, and half-truths leap from ready mouths to eager ears. The dancing flames of gossip enliven conversations as people gather around its hot, tantalizing fire, bonded by the excitement of being among those who know.

Like a glowing ember in a forest of dry trees, the fire of gossip is far from harmless. One idly dropped spark has the potential to set off a blaze that sears a person's dignity and reputation. Its smoke strangles cautious voices and obstructs fair thinking. Gossip radiates the light of knowledge, although it never stops leaping long enough to check for facts. Gossip exudes togetherness but results in divided loyalties, prejudice, distrust, and suspicion.

God calls gossip a sin. It directly breaks two of His Ten Commandments—do not steal and do not give false testimony. Gossip indiscriminately takes reputation and dignity without reasons clearly based on a person's behavior. Gossip arbitrarily accuses without definite proof or plain evidence. In addition, gossip violates God's command to treat others the way you would like them to treat you. It thwarts the promptings of His Spirit toward well-considered and kindly speech. Indeed, half-truths and untruths have no place in the lives of those who worship the God of all truth.

Don't fan the flame of gossip by repeating it. If the information concerns something that needs your attention, get the facts and then take necessary and appropriate action. Carefully keep sensitive matters concerning others on a need-to-know basis, respecting their privacy as you would like them to respect yours. Avoid the hot glare of gossip. Instead, stand in the cool light of truth.

> *Fire goes out for lack of fuel,*
> *and quarrels disappear when gossip stops.*
> PROVERBS 26:20 NLT

THE WORLD SAYS:
"Men are superior to women."

GOD SAYS:
"In My kingdom, there is no male or female, slave or free."

In Christ's family there can be no division into Jew and non-Jew, slave and free, male and female. Among us you are all equal. That is, we are all in a common relationship with Jesus Christ.

GALATIANS 3:28 MSG

Christians are one in Christ. Earthly distinctions disappear under the shadow of His cross, and social standing means nothing in front of the throne of heaven. No nationality receives precedence over another. No person's gender or ethnicity attracts approval or suffers scorn. All worldly measures of rank and rights vanish in God's eyes.

In baptism, God brings about the equality of all believers. Baptism clothes believers in the robe of Christ's righteousness, which means everyone's dressed the same in the kingdom of heaven—a sad fact for fashion designers, but an indescribable comfort to anyone who has ever felt slighted or discriminated against because of race, rank, or gender. Baptism confers a status far outranking anything the world can offer or anyone can personally achieve. Through the power of the Holy Spirit through baptism, God clothes you in Christ's pure garment and delights to call you His beloved child.

The biblical account of Nicodemus's nighttime visit to Jesus illustrates the point. Nicodemus, a distinguished scholar and religious leader, acknowledged Jesus' miracles. But Jesus cut to the finish. "You need to be born again," He told His astonished guest. "You need to be born of water and Spirit before you can enter the kingdom of God" (see John 3:5). Nicodemus's high status in the world had nothing to do with his status in the kingdom of God. Only God's work in him, through water and Spirit, could elevate Nicodemus to his place in God's kingdom.

When you pray, God doesn't care if you're kneeling in a palace or a prison. He's not running a background check on you before deciding how He'll relate to you. No matter who you are, you'll get the same reception as every other Christ-covered believer: "Welcome, My beloved child. Welcome."

Accept one another, then, just as Christ accepted you, in order to bring praise to God.

ROMANS 15:7

THE WORLD SAYS:
"Some races are superior to others."

GOD SAYS:
"Each person is precious and created in My image."

So God created people in his own image; God patterned them after himself; male and female he created them.

GENESIS 1:27 NLT

In Jesus' day, racism separated Jews and Samaritans. Since Samaria lay between the Jewish regions of Judea and Galilee, pious Jewish travelers customarily detoured well east of Samaria to avoid contact with the despised people. Not Jesus. Leaving Judea in the south and heading north to Galilee, He took the shortest route—right through Samaria.

During one trip, Jesus arrived at a place in Samaria now called Jacob's Well. He sat down and rested there. Shortly, a Samaritan woman came to draw water. The woman had no reason to think He would even acknowledge her, being a woman and a Samaritan. The Lord, however, asked her for a cup of water. Imagine the woman's astonishment! Once a conversation got started, Jesus took the opportunity to speak to her of His living water…the wellspring of eternal life…the Word of God.

God sent Jesus for the salvation of the world. Racial prejudices and ethnic hostilities crumble before the all-embracing love of God. He invites everyone, of every nation and of every ethnic group. By the well in Samaria, Jesus set an example for all His disciples.

Racial superiority and ethnic favoritism carry no currency in the kingdom of God. Such discrimination should have no place in the lives of believers, either. Unfortunately, prejudices of society often permeate the church. Some individuals feel unwelcome in certain churches, and racially mixed congregations remain all too few. Tragically, some souls have turned to God, only to be turned away by God's people.

Examine your thoughts, outlook, and actions. Do you harbor negative opinions of one race of people because of the actions of a few? Do you fail to see the positive qualities of someone because of his or her nationality, background, hometown, or address? Picture that person in your mind right now. Ask God to give you eyes to recognize His image in everyone—including him. Including her.

Jesus said, "I pray also for those who will believe in me.…
May they be brought to complete unity to let the world know
that you sent me."

JOHN 17:20, 23

THE WORLD SAYS:
"Cheating on your taxes is okay—it doesn't hurt anybody."

GOD SAYS:
"Don't be deceived. Whatever you sow, you will also reap."

You cannot fool God, so don't make a fool of yourself! You will harvest what you plant.
Galatians 6:7 CEV

To make the honor roll, a student cheats on examinations. To land the job, an applicant lists phony credentials. To lower a tax bill, an entrepreneur pads business expenses. Each soothes the stab of conscience by insisting, "What I did hurts no one." Each smiles in satisfaction at being clever enough to work the system to his or her advantage.

Seemingly minor "victimless" acts of cheating stealthily worm their way into daily practice. Little instances of trickery pass unnoticed by anyone and establish themselves as habit. Ask yourself: *When there's little chance of being caught, do I cheat? If I could easily explain away or cover up an act of deception, would I go ahead with it?* Cheating, even cheating never detected by anyone, cannot hide from a holy God who sees inside the heart. Through self-justification or denial, trivial deceit edges out the Holy Spirit, clearing the way for more daring schemes...more elaborate hoaxes...more sophisticated methods of cheating.

Cheating is an offense against God, and it's also an offense against yourself. No cheater possesses the serenity of a clear conscience. No cheater can take real pride in his or her accomplishments, knowing the honors, privileges, or benefits were not honestly earned. No cheater can be sure others will not discover his or her deception and reveal it for all to see. No cheater handles big responsibilities honestly because so many small ones were accomplished in dishonest ways. No cheater obtains God's peace because dishonesty denies the Spirit of truth. Cheating always takes victims—the first one being the cheater.

Regardless of the level of cheating you have engaged in, turn to your Lord and Savior in repentance. He suffered, died, and rose again to win your redemption, and He waits right now to bring you His forgiveness, comfort, and peace.

Jesus said, "Whoever can be trusted with very little can also be trusted with much, and whoever is dishonest with very little will also be dishonest with much."

LUKE 16:10

THE WORLD SAYS:
"I'm the boss of my own life."

GOD SAYS:
"One day, every knee will bow and every tongue will confess that Jesus Christ is Lord."

Then God gave Christ the highest place and honored his name above all others. So at the name of Jesus everyone will bow down, those in heaven, on earth, and under the earth. And to the glory of God the Father everyone will openly agree, "Jesus Christ is Lord!"

PHILIPPIANS 2:9–11 CEV

Self-help books fill many feet of shelf space in bookstores. Titles from this category spend weeks on the nation's list of best-sellers. Readers want to know how to control their lives—the right steps to take, the right things to say, the right people to know.

Quality self-help titles can aid readers in determining goals and discovering practical ways to reach those goals. A couple of problems arise, though, when readers believe their goals, plans, and opportunities are theirs alone to decide. First, what a burden they give themselves. Imagine having to second-guess your every move, wondering if you took exactly the step you needed to take for ultimate success. Second, what an ego. Even secular observers leave plenty of room for "fate," "luck," and "chance." It doesn't take a Bible-thumper to realize the folly inherent in presuming to control one's destiny.

Jesus came to serve people. He served in practical ways through His ministry of teaching and healing. He served in spiritual ways through His ministry of compassion and forgiveness. As the Risen Christ, He continues to serve through the ministry of the church and His intercession on behalf of all believers. He is Lord of all, King of kings, yet He served and continues to serve.

His followers have His example to emulate. Give control of your life to the One who's the Creator of your life. Use the perspective He gives you to discern those things He has put under your control and those things He has retained under His control.

Clear thinking and smart strategies can help you make the most of the blessings He has given you. Take full advantage of His gifts by developing your talents and skills to the glory of God. But in all things, remember who you are—a beloved servant of the One who has first served you.

Submit yourselves therefore to God.
JAMES 4:7 NRSV

THE WORLD SAYS:
"One person can't make a difference."

GOD SAYS:
"You and I together can change the world."

*Two are better than one, because
they have a good return for their work.*

ECCLESIASTES 4:9

In the early years of the Christian church, the aging missionary Paul mentored young Timothy in the ways of church leadership. Timothy, perhaps comparing his rank inexperience to Paul's awesome achievements, suffered from acute insecurity. Paul wrote to Timothy: "Allow no one to despise you because you're young. Focus on God's Word. Do God's work" (see 1 Timothy 4:12–13). While Timothy saw what he *couldn't* do for God, Paul was looking at what God *could* do with Timothy.

When do you succumb to Timothy-like lack of confidence? *Yes, Lord,* you say to yourself, *I'd do this for You except that I'm…* Then you name the one big bugaboo hovering over you. Too young. Not experienced. Too old. Trained in another field. Certain to fail. Afraid of making a fool out of yourself. *And I couldn't possibly make much of a difference anyway.*

If you focus honestly on your own abilities, you're bound for discouragement. If you decide to tackle the world's ills by yourself, you're headed for frustration. But if you look to the God who has called you, you will begin to see changes in yourself. You will begin to see opportunities right around you where you can make a difference. Perhaps there's a family member longing for someone to ask about her day. Or a friend who's feeling down in the dumps right now. Or a church committee or charity desperately in need of volunteers. Or a community project begging for someone's energy and attention. All these things and more are possible. Maybe you won't change the world. But over time, the world—and you—will see some remarkable changes.

A sign posted on a church's bulletin board reads: "God doesn't call the qualified. He qualifies the called." Ask God about your qualifications today.

It was [God] who gave some to be apostles, some to be prophets, some to be evangelists, and some to be pastors and teachers, to prepare God's people for works of service.

Ephesians 4:11–12

THE WORLD SAYS:
"I can't go on—I'm too weak."

GOD SAYS:
"My strength is made perfect in your weakness."

[God] gives strength to the weary and increases the power of the weak.

ISAIAH 40:29

As parents know, children will not develop strength of character if the parents make everything easy for them. Youngsters learn the value of nothing if parents give them everything they demand, and they never learn to reach if everything falls into their lap. Children will never internalize ethical principles if adults solve every external problem for them. Through years of training, practice, seeing, and doing, the tenuous abilities of a child develop into the strong character of an adult.

In much the same way, the Holy Spirit works with and through your weaknesses to develop and strengthen your spiritual character. Obvious weaknesses of the flesh and of the world point to the universal need for deliverance, a deliverance strong enough to defeat the power of sin—Jesus Christ. Your faith in Jesus' deliverance gives you His strength. "But," you protest, "I still sin. I'm still weak."

While Jesus' sacrifice on your behalf has lifted you from the damning consequences of sin, you still sin. You're still weak. That's wonderful—really! Let His Spirit now use your weakness to the advantage of your spiritual character. Be patient with Him, for He guides you with the tender concern of a loving parent. Maybe you don't understand why you struggle constantly with a particular sin; maybe you can't imagine how your weaknesses could ever benefit you or anyone else. Neither does a child know all the ways of a parent.

When you feel your weaknesses weighing in with too much force, lighten them with a visit with your heavenly Father. Let His Word instruct you. Let His presence assist you. Let His promptings give you the confidence to stick with yourself...to try again...to keep on going, weaknesses and all. Then prepare to notice a new muscle in the character of your spirit.

My flesh and my heart may fail, but God is the strength of my heart and my portion forever.

PSALM 73:26

THE WORLD SAYS:
"Give up—there is no hope."

GOD SAYS:
"Put your hope in Me, and you will not be disappointed."

Wisdom is sweet to your soul; if you find it, there is a future hope for you, and your hope will not be cut off.

PROVERBS 24:14

When the future looks dismal to you, what do you do? Some people sit wringing their hands while they loudly bewail the state of the world. Others sulk, seething with anger toward the people or circumstances they blame for their bleak prospects, and still others sink into depression, unshakably certain the future holds no hope for them.

God knows how scary the future can look to human eyes. After a string of failures, setbacks, and disappointments, human reasoning predicts more of the same in the days, years, and decades ahead. Shocking national and world events leave little doubt of the challenging times ahead. Devastating personal circumstances with lifelong consequences cloud even the most optimistic outlook. God knows—and He answers.

The prophet Jeremiah preached in the years leading up to the fall of Jerusalem in 586 BC. Under God's direction, Jeremiah presented a gloomy forecast for the people of Judah. As a result of their persistent godlessness and disobedience, God would allow a foreign power to destroy Jerusalem and take a goodly part of the population into captivity. God's terrible punishment, however, came not without hope. In their exile, He would be with them, ready and willing to hear their prayers of repentance and petition. Disaster loomed on the horizon, yes…but God would work it out for the well-being of His people. He had good plans for them; He declared. "Do not give up hope. Set your eyes on Me."

God speaks these same words to you today. You might find yourself held captive by any number of personal struggles, family situations, and national or world circumstances. But God has not forgotten you, nor does He plan bad things for you. He offers you hope and a future. Why not ask Him about it now?

Be strong and take heart, all you who hope in the LORD.
PSALM 31:24

TRUTH.

THE WORLD SAYS:
"Seek financial security."

GOD SAYS:
"Money cannot provide security. Only My love can do that."

You're my cave to hide in, my cliff to climb.
Be my safe leader, be my true mountain guide.

PSALM 31:3 MSG

Responsible people pay attention to their finances. In anticipation of a comfortable retirement, young people begin putting money aside as soon as their earning years begin. Families budget their income and make sacrifices now for the sake of the future. Retirees often find part-time employment to supplement their savings.

Financial security brings with it many benefits—comfortable living, the ability to enjoy hobbies and recreational activities, the means to meet unexpected expenses, and the freedom to make agreeable lifestyle choices. Trouble rears its ugly head, however, when financial security morphs into spiritual security.

Money's power is limited. Just ask a multimillion-dollar lottery winner who finds himself in debt after five years. Ask a wealthy executive whose empire comes crashing down in the wake of a financial scandal. Ask an investor whose stocks and bonds have plummeted, along with hopes and dreams for a secure future. When people look to money for ultimate security, it fails miserably.

God gives you true security for free. It's called grace. God's love reaches you through your faith in Jesus Christ and His work for your salvation. Nothing you have spent, saved, earned, or found has anything to do with the grace of God who has chosen you. God's economy rests on love—His love.

Now might be a good time to review your finances. On what do you spend the most money? Why? What do you hope to gain with your actual or potential investment portfolio? Are you loading your money down with expectations of security it can't buy you? Talk to God about your money. After all, He gave it to you. Ask Him to help you put money in its proper place and your relationship with Him in its proper place. He'll know exactly how to advise you.

Listen, you who say, "Today or tomorrow we will go to this or that city, spend a year there, carry on business and make money." Why, you do not even know what will happen tomorrow.

JAMES 4:13–14

THE WORLD SAYS:
"I don't know how to talk to God."

GOD SAYS:
"I'm not impressed by fancy words. I see the intent of the heart."

God has surely listened and heard my voice in prayer. Praise be to God, who has not rejected my prayer or withheld his love from me!
PSALM 66:19–20

The book of Psalms ranks as one of the most read and most beloved books of the Bible. Its hymns, poems, and prayers range in emotion from deepest agony of body and mind to highest ecstasy of joy and thanksgiving. The psalms express emotions—including anger, fear, and vengeance—in vibrant, unvarnished terms. For many Christians, Psalms is their daily prayer book.

Rather than focusing on specific words or set formulas for prayer, the psalms teach something far more important—an attitude toward prayer. The psalmist went before God boldly, but humbly. He addressed God Almighty who must (and will) bend down to hear the words of His creatures. Throughout the psalms, the psalmist expressed his trust in God, even in those times when events challenged such trust. Why? Because doubtful prayer is no prayer at all. The psalmist's frequent cries to God to save him reveal God's solution for flagging trust: Ask Him for more trust.

The psalmist prayed faithfully. Many psalms attest to his habit of daily prayer, his constant presence before God's throne, his tireless meditation on God's words and commandments. His example leads the way for all believers to approach God regularly, not just when trouble comes or a convenient time turns up. God intends that His people talk to Him every day with their words of praise, petition, and thanksgiving.

Thanksgiving—how often has God not heard a word of thanks for blessings He has given? In contrast, the psalmist often gives thanks to God even before God has answered the prayer! His gratitude reveals his faith in the power and effectiveness of prayer—prayer offered daily in an attitude of humility, trust, faithfulness, and gratitude.

In prayer, your words may be those of the Bible, church tradition, an inspirational writer, or those spoken from the depths of your heart. Whatever words you use, pray humbly …pray trustingly…pray daily…pray thankfully.

"Before they call I will answer; while they are still speaking I will hear," says the Lord.

Isaiah 65:24–25

THE WORLD SAYS:
"I'm not worthy of God's love."

GOD SAYS:
"My love has made you worthy."

*If God says his chosen ones are acceptable to him,
can anyone bring charges against them?*

ROMANS 8:33 CEV

A parable has been defined as an earthly story with a heavenly meaning. In one parable, Jesus tells about a wealthy father who has two sons. At one point, the younger son demands of his father the inheritance due him. He receives it, bundles up his money and possessions, and goes out to live the good life. The inevitable happens, of course. He soon spends everything he has and ends up slopping pigs to live. Deep in the muck of the sty, the son remembers his father. He decides to return, repent, and beg to reenter his father's house as a servant.

Unknown to the young man, his father has been out every day watching for him to return. Before he even reaches the door of the house, his father rushes out to meet him. The father tearfully embraces his returned son. He calls for a ring, a robe, and sandals for the boy. He takes his son into the house with celebration and joy.

Human worthiness plays no role in our Father's love, as Jesus' parable illustrates. God delights in receiving back even the most wayward sinner, waiting for confession, repentance, and return. He welcomes His people as sons…as daughters. He rushes out to meet them with the ring, robe, and sandals of Jesus' righteousness.

The wayward son approached his father with the intention of demanding something of his father—again. This time, he wanted to join the family as a servant. False humility tempts the repentant sinner to make a similar demand, offering terms to God for His acceptance. As the wayward son's father had other plans, so does your heavenly Father. No matter which "pigsty" you're in or you've just stepped out of, you're His son or His daughter. Such is the Father's will. Such is your Father's love.

Now your sins have been washed away, and you have been set apart for God. You have been made right with God because of what the Lord Jesus Christ and the Spirit of our God have done for you.

1 Corinthians 6:11 nlt

THE WORLD SAYS:
"Crime pays."

GOD SAYS:
"The wages of sin is death."

*Sin pays off with death. But God's gift is eternal life
given by Jesus Christ our Lord.*

ROMANS 6:23 CEV

Some readers use the Bible as a source of sound principles for living. Certain commonly repeated maxims and proverbs come from the pages of scripture and are accepted by the world as good rules to follow. Indeed, many adherents of religions outside Christianity respect Jesus as a saintly prophet and wise teacher. Unfortunately, this kind of thinking misses the point of biblical advice and guidance. It's not just to keep people away from criminal activity, but to keep believers from eternal death by grace through faith in Jesus.

Grace has been defined as the undeserved love of God for undeserving sinners. When sinners attempt to win God's love by trying to follow His rules and commandments to the letter, they end up (sadly and ironically) without knowing God's love. God loves because of grace, and earned love is not grace—it's payment due. Outside God's grace, sinners receive their self-earned reward—death.

God's grace took on human form in the person of Jesus Christ. In His life on Earth, He did what no one else could do—that is, He followed God's rules and commandments to the letter. Perfectly. Without fault or error. He fulfilled God's grace-filled plan for the salvation of the world by giving Himself as full and complete payment for the wages of sin. He didn't do it because anyone deserved it. He did it because of grace.

God's grace didn't stop with Jesus' victory over death. It's not a set commodity plopped into your soul at the moment of your baptism, nor is it a once-in-a-lifetime spiritual event. By contrast, the awareness of God's grace grows in you as you grow in His Word. Grace lifts you upward in your spiritual growth as you gain godly experience and sanctified maturity.

God's grace frees you from the wages of sin, which is death, and frees you for the rewards of service, which is life—eternal life.

Come near to God and he will come near to you. Wash your hands, you sinners, and purify your hearts, you double-minded.... Humble yourselves before the Lord, and he will lift you up.

JAMES 4:8, 10

THE WORLD SAYS:
"God has forsaken me."

GOD SAYS:
"I will never leave you nor forsake you."

Don't be obsessed with getting more material things. Be relaxed with what you have. Since God assured us, "I'll never let you down, never walk off and leave you."

HEBREWS 13:5 MSG

Every once in a while, someone reveals himself or herself to be a fair-weather friend. When you provide upbeat, cheerful, and lively companionship, the person's a ready and reliable buddy. But should you need someone to listen, someone to help you through a rough time, someone to just be there for you, your good-time pal disappears. He's too busy to come over. She'd love to listen, but…some other time, okay?

Christians often treat God as just that kind of friend—a fair-weather friend. Under bright, clear skies—good health, great job, wonderful relationships—prayers of thanksgiving gush from smiling lips. When setbacks cloud the sky, however, gratitude disappears from the forecast. An unexpected and unprepared-for layoff rains on a sunny financial future. Medical tests confirm the worst-case diagnosis. Divorce. Loss. A low, dark cloud spans from horizon to horizon, as far as the eye can see.

Where is God? Based on some human relationships, it's natural to conclude that He doesn't stick around when it's raining. After all, a catastrophe has happened to you. This life-altering event has intruded, and God isn't providing an escape. He isn't answering in any expected way, so it must mean He's not listening. And He's not listening because He's not here. He's gone.

In His true and reliable Word, God assures you He will never leave you, not under any circumstances. He is not a fair-weather friend, but an ever-present Friend who never permits a trial to touch you without providing you with the strength to go through it. He may—or may not—bring back the sunshine today, or even tomorrow. At such times, do not forsake Him, but draw closer to Him, lean on Him, and depend on His promise to be there…to listen…to care. Your Friend has given you His Word.

Be strong and courageous! Do not be afraid of them! The Lord your God will go ahead of you. He will neither fail you nor forsake you.
DEUTERONOMY 31:6 NLT

THE WORLD SAYS:
"I want to believe in God, but I lack faith."

GOD SAYS:
"Faith comes by hearing, and hearing by the word of God."

Consequently, faith comes from hearing the message, and the message is heard through the word of Christ.

Romans 10:17

If you can say, "I want to believe in God," the Holy Spirit has planted in you the seed of faith. Now what?

In His parable about a farmer scattering seeds, Jesus speaks about the seed of faith scattered by the Word of God. Some of the farmer's seed falls on the packed-down dirt of the road. What seeds passersby don't trample down, birds snatch up. This is like the Word of God falling on the ears of hearers too busy to listen, too hurried to hear more. Quickly, the seed of faith gets snatched up by worldly concerns.

Some of the farmer's seed lands among rocks where it germinates in crevices and begins to take root. Shortly, the seedlings wither for lack of water. This happens when hearers gladly listen and eagerly believe, but they don't put down roots among other believers. They don't join a church. They don't commit to discipleship. For lack of roots, their faith wilts at the first hot wind of testing. Other seed falls in thorn-infested soil and is promptly choked out by weeds. This seed describes hearers who accept the Word of God gladly, but they let personal pleasures, lusts, and worries overrun the seed of faith.

Some of the farmer's seed falls on good, rich, fertile soil. This seed grows and produces an abundant harvest. This is the Word of God that comes to hearers who listen to it, hold on to it, and continue in it. Faith, rooted in the deep, rich soil of God's Word, grows strong and vibrant. Nurtured by the Holy Spirit, it produces an abundant harvest of love, joy, and peace.

His Spirit has sown the Word of God in you, for you have heard Him say: "Believe in Jesus Christ, the One I sent to take away your sins." What will the Farmer find when He checks on His crop today?

The seed on good soil stands for those with a noble and good heart, who hear the word, retain it, and by persevering produce a crop.

LUKE 8:15

TRUTH.

THE WORLD SAYS:
"God doesn't heal people anymore."

GOD SAYS:
"I am the same yesterday, today, and forever."

Jesus doesn't change—yesterday, today, tomorrow, he's always totally himself.
HEBREWS 13:8 MSG

Far too many Christians soft-pedal or flatly deny the miracles of the Bible. Skeptical theologians teach that healings, resurrections, calmed storms, and multiplied fish merely symbolize spiritual truths. In this scientific age, miracles are dismissed as relics of credulous people in gullible times.

God, however, has not dismissed Himself from miracles. Throughout the Bible, He revealed His power by suspending the laws of nature—after all, He defined those laws in the first place! God in Jesus Christ used miracles to attest to His divine nature and authority. His many healings of body and mind proved His credentials as the Messiah, the One God had promised in the Garden of Eden. To deny miracles denies His divinity…His resurrection from the dead…His ability and authority to forgive sins and promise eternal life. To deny miracles denies the core of the Christian faith.

Jesus gave His apostles the power to perform miracles of healing in the early years of the church. As a sign of the apostles' gospel mission, miracles served to defend and strengthen a nascent and often persecuted church. Though the church, now well established, has no need of miraculous healings to prove God's presence, no one should restrict God by saying what He can and can't do. He certainly may effect a healing without evident means, and many believers can personally attest to His miraculous power. Generally, however, when someone receives healing, He works through the means of modern medicine, medical procedures, and the healing arts of today. Is that any less miraculous? To the many He has healed that way, the answer would be a resounding no!

Indeed, God heals. Faith itself is the greatest miracle of healing ever. He invites you to let Him heal you of your wounds and touch you with His balm for forgiveness and peace. A miracle? You can answer that!

The prayer offered in faith will make the sick person well;
the Lord will raise him up.

JAMES 5:15

THE WORLD SAYS:
"Prayer has no place in the classroom."

GOD SAYS:
"Have you seen what has happened in the classroom since prayer was removed?"

Keep on praying.
1 Thessalonians 5:17 nlt

"There will always be prayer in the classroom," an observer remarked wryly, "as long as there are algebra tests." The complexity of algebra and the certainty of tests aside, prayer has a place wherever Christians find themselves. In the face of religious diversity, however, faculty-sponsored prayer has been removed from public school classrooms.

The exclusion of prayer and religious symbols from schools, workplaces, public buildings, and recreation areas reflects the secularization of society. The trend dismays many Christians, who fear for the quality of community life. But the trend away from "public" Christianity signals a call—a requirement—for "private" Christians to take on new challenges and responsibilities.

Without relying on teachers, the state, or the government to put a public face on Christianity, individual Christians must challenge themselves to learn—and their churches to teach—the full counsel of God. Outside the church, it's no one's job to teach you Bible truths or lead you in prayer. You cannot expect to have your beliefs bolstered in the public arena. Motivated and enabled by His Spirit, you're challenged to build and maintain a deep, strong faith.

As public expression of Christianity decreases, individual Christian witness must increase. In public forums, Christians have the responsibility to uphold Christian values and support biblical truths. Gone are the days of assumed Christianity. Your neighbors may not know of Jesus beyond a sweet infant lying in a manger. Your coworkers may hear the word *Easter* and think of eggs and bunnies. Your classmates may neither know how to pray nor to whom.

The world's voice calls for an end to prayer in the classrooms and many other places. The Spirit's voice calls for the beginning of renewed energy on the part of Christians wherever they are. How and where will He use your voice, your presence, your actions to bring God's love to others today?

What other nation is so great as to have their gods near them the way the LORD our God is near us whenever we pray to him?
DEUTERONOMY 4:7

THE WORLD SAYS:
"Death is the end."

GOD SAYS:
"You will live eternally—the question is where?"

Jesus said to his disciples, "Don't be worried! Have faith in God and have faith in me. There are many rooms in my Father's house. I wouldn't tell you this, unless it was true. I am going there to prepare a place for each of you."

JOHN 14:1–2 CEV

The world prefers to ignore death because the world simply lacks an adequate answer to death's question: What lies beyond the grave?

Non-Christians have little to hope for in the face of death. No surprise here—they have never grasped the purpose of life. Their ambitions and values crumble under vague notions of a hereafter expressed in platitudes and quasi-religious sentiments. As they see it, death is the end. Right—the end of human knowledge. God in Jesus Christ can see what lies beyond the grave because He's been there.

The certainty of heaven and hell—of salvation and damnation—stems from the Bible's clear and repeated references to both places. In God's Word, He clearly and un-equivocally speaks of hell and damnation awaiting those who refuse His gospel invitation. Does He send people to hell? No. People send themselves there by choosing self over God.

The Bible with equal clarity and firmness speaks of heaven and eternal life in God's presence for those who come to Him through Jesus Christ. Heaven has nothing to do with how good you are or anything you have done for Him or will do for Him in the future. It has to do with grace—God's grace to you through the life, death, and resurrection of Jesus Christ. By grace through faith in Jesus, you have the kingdom of heaven.

Knowing with certainty what's ahead for you, you can confidently and joyfully serve Him right now. He has freed you from the condemnation of sin. He has given your life meaning and purpose. He has opened your eyes to His Spirit at work in you. You have nothing to fear from death because your faith has put your life—your physical life and your spiritual life—in His hands.

If the earthly tent we live in is destroyed, we have a building from God, an eternal house in heaven, not built by human hands.

2 CORINTHIANS 5:1

TRUTH NEVER DIES

Truth never dies.
The ages come and go;
The mountains wear away; the seas retire;
Destruction lays earth's mighty cities low;
And empires, states, and dynasties expire;
But caught and handed onward by the wise,
Truth never dies.

Though unreceived and scoffed at through the years;
Though made the butt of ridicule and jest;
Though held aloft for mockery and jeers,
Denied by those of transient power possessed,
Insulted by the insolence of lies,
Truth never dies.

Truth answers not; it does not take offense:
But with mighty silence bides its time.
As some great cliff that braves the elements,
And lifts through all the storms its head sublime,
So truth, unmoved, its puny foes defies,
And never dies!

AUTHOR UNKNOWN

Also Available from Barbour Publishing

Why listen to what the world says
about sex, love, and marriage,
when you can get God's point of view?

Sex.
Discovering Real Love in a World of Counterfeits
1-59789-134-7

Available Fall 2006
Wherever Books Are Sold.